Issues in Canadian/U.S. Transborder Computer Data Flows

edited by
W.E. Cundiff
and
Mado Reid

Proceedings of a conference held
in Montreal at the Four Seasons Hotel
and sponsored by the
Institute for Research on Public Policy
September 6, 1978

Institute for Research on Public Policy/Institut de recherches politiques

Distributed by
Butterworth & Co. (Canada) Ltd.
Toronto

© 1979 Institute for Research on Public Policy
All rights reserved

ISBN 0 920380 12 3

Legal Deposit First Quarter
Bibliothèque nationale du Québec

Institute for Research on Public Policy/Institut de recherches politiques
3535, chemin Queen Mary, Bureau 514
Montréal, Québec H3V 1H8

Preface

Because of advances in computer communications, many experts are forecasting a global communications revolution that will see the processing of information as the principal activity of a post-industrial society. However, while great technological advances in such areas as satellite communications, computer networking, and microprocessor chips are occurring at a seemingly unlimited pace, recent developments in the regulation of the flow of information across national boundaries may lead to severe restrictions on the true "globalization" of information technology. Indeed, with the rapid growth in the information sector of the world economy, nations are starting to institute measures which will enable them to gain maximum economic benefit from this new industry and build domestic capability in information processing.

It is the fear of many associated with international computer communications that policy makers are acting too hastily in the establishment of barriers to the free flow of data. In fact, because of the extraordinary pace of technological change, it appears that many laws have been enacted without a thorough analysis of their implications for industry or the general public.

The goal of IRPP research in transborder data flows is to help policy makers and the information processing community appreciate the various factors which must be considered in developing transborder data flow policies. This is particularly important in the Canadian context, because other countries are looking to the way in which transborder data flow between Canada and the United States as a model for what should happen elsewhere in the world.

                                               Michael J.L. Kirby
                                               President
                                               December 1978

Préface

En raison de l'essor des communications informatiques, de nombreux experts prévoient un bouleversement radical des communications qui placera le traitement de l'information au premier rang des activités de la société post-industrielle. Toutefois, alors que de grands progrès technologiques, dans des domaines tels que les communications par satellite, la mise sur pied de réseaux informatiques et les micro-unités de traitement, se succèdent à un rythme quasi effréné, les développements récents de la réglementation de la circulation des informations au-delà des frontières nationales peuvent mener à de sévères restrictions sur la centralisation véritable de la technologie de l'information. En fait, étant donnée la croissance rapide du secteur de l'information dans l'économie mondiale, les nations commencent à prendre des dispositions pour s'assurer qu'elles tireront le maximum d'avantages économiques de cette nouvelle industrie et bâtiront leur propre système de traitement de l'information.

Les personnes associées au domaine des communications informatiques internationales craignent que les responsables de l'élaboration des politiques n'agissent trop à la légère en dressant des barrières au libre écoulement des données. De fait, à cause du rythme extraordinaire auquel change la technologie, il semble que plusieurs lois ont été édictées sans qu'on ait mesuré avec précision leurs implications pour l'industrie ou le public en général.

Par ses travaux, l'IRP cherche à aider les responsables de la conception des politiques, de même que les personnes rattachées au domaine de l'informatique, à comprendre les divers facteurs qui doivent être pris en considération dans l'élaboration des politiques en matière de transmission de données outre-frontières. Ce travail s'avère particulièrement important dans le contexte canadien, puisqu'aux yeux des autres pays, la circulation des données au-delà des frontières canado-américaines illustre les tendances susceptibles de se manifester ailleurs dans le monde.

Michael J.L. Kirby
Président
Décembre 1978

Table of Contents

Preface ....*by Michael J.L. Kirby* iii

Introduction ....*by David Hoffman* 1

Chapter One Issues in Canadian/U.S. Transborder
Computer Data Flows ....*by W.E. Cundiff* 11

Chapter Two Panel Discussion and Response to the Issues
.........*by Morris Crawford, George Fierheller, Dr. Peter Robinson,*
....*J.C. Grant, Brendan McShane, Andrew McMahon, John M. Eger* 33

Chapter Three Comments of Participants 63

Chapter Four Workshop Reports and Commentary 65

Appendix 1: Position Statements 73

Appendix 2: List of Participants 85

Introduction

by
David Hoffman
Institute for Research on Public Policy

The conference/workshop, whose proceedings the Institute for Research on Public Policy is publishing, originated in a research project within the Futures Studies program. Zavis P. Zeman, project leader responsible for a series of probes into future impacts on Canada of technological and economic changes, Bill Cundiff, senior research associate, and Robert Russel, then consultant-editor working for the program, began their thinking about the subject with a relatively simple framework. They would identify the new technological developments working to facilitate transborder computer data flows, and assess the social, and particularly the economic, consequences for Canada if observed trends continued or even accelerated. The main issue, as it emerged in Bill Cundiff's working paper, was not the flow of data so much as the movement across borders of the jobs related to the processing of the data. To be more precise—since the predictable direction of the flow was North to South rather than the reverse—the question became: what are the implications for the loss of jobs and the erosion of job opportunities in Canada?

Describing the technological innovation was relatively easy; assessing the economic impacts—even the historical record, to say nothing of speculating about future developments—was more difficult. The excellent work on the subject done by the now-disbanded Computer/Communications Secretariat in the federal Department of Communications was available. However, after careful analysis of the data, it was concluded that the surveys on which the analysis was based drew from such a small sample that it was impossible to infer long-term trends. In particular, the time-series data exhibited cyclical fluctuations which made it difficult to fit curves to them. Therefore, any projection of the curves into the longer term seemed risky. Nevertheless, there was sufficient evidence that the issues should not be ignored.

One of the conclusions of the research probe—for which we hoped, frankly, to get endorsement from the conference participants—was that a fuller survey than any that exists at the moment is necessary in order to establish the facts; that a survey of computing practices of the major corporations in Canada is essential to provide the badly needed data on which policy analysis, and subsequent policy, might be dealt. Readers of these *Proceedings* will see that we received support for our contention from only a minority of the conference participants.

The original perspective of Bill Cundiff's study was technology driven, that is, the rapid expansion of computer communications, facilitated by new developments such as packet switching, satellites, and the linking of U.S.-based telecommunications networks with Bell Canada's Datapac network, was seen to have consequences arising from the fact that data are transmitted in such a way that they could not easily be made subject to normal customs clearance or other controls. However, as the research deepened, it became clear that the centralizing of accounting, auditing, and data processing in American parent firms may be due less to new, cheap technology than to particular management styles. This is associated with the international structure of the companies in question. Those firms which are "miniature replicas" engaged in production of only a small segment of the products of the American parent company are less likely to send their major computing activities back to head office. This analysis reinforced the feeling that an elaborate survey which took structural variables into account would be necessary.

The focus on the economic implications, rather than the related issue of privacy, proved to be a key determinant in the subsequent decision to use the research results as the basis for organizing an international conference. The candor evident in directly attacking the main issue appeared attractive on both sides of the border, and Bill Cundiff returned from the American Federation of Information Processing Societies' (AFIPS) 1978 National Computer Conference in Anaheim, California convinced that the issue was ripe for discussion. Events soon proved him right. As one conference participant, Oswald Ganley from Harvard University, put it: "This . . . is the first meeting where we have cast away the screen of privacy that has been hanging over these discussions over the last two years, and where we are frankly facing the facts that what we are really talking about are important economic and cultural questions."

In order to represent a broad range of perspectives to conference participants, a panel of experts was created, consisting of the following:
— Morris Crawford, Acting Director, Office of Bilateral and Multilateral Science and Technology Programs, U.S. Department of State, Washington, D.C.
— John M. Eger, Attorney-at-Law, Washington, D.C.
— George Fierheller, President, Systems Dimensions Ltd., Ottawa
— J.C. Grant, Assistant General Manager, Systems Development, Royal Bank of Canada, Montreal
— A.M. McMahon, Vice-President, Computer Communications, Bell Canada, Ottawa
— Brendan McShane, Consulting Specialist on Information Services, Bethesda
— Dr. Peter Robinson, Policy Adviser, Computer/Communications, Department of Communications, Ottawa

Each panelist was invited to prepare in advance a set of brief remarks on the issue of transborder data flows. These were collected together and sent, along with a copy of the working paper, to all who subscribed to the conference. In this way, the participants could proceed from the basic position statements already made by the panelists, as well as the institute's research report, which became the basis of Bill Cundiff's keynote address. As expected, this procedure led to quick confrontation of the key issues, for following the address, the panelists immediately began to comment on each other's previously stated positions.

In the afternoon, the sixty-odd participants divided into four workshops, presided over by panelists who also served as rapporteurs. The discussion was to centre around five areas of potential danger rising from transnational computer communications, identified by the then minister of state for Science and Technology, J. Hugh Faulkner, in the summer of 1977. One of the groups, in the words of its rapporteur, "had a wide-ranging, free-for-all, no-holds-barred sort of discussion" and did not stick to the plan; but the other three tried to focus on those five areas:

1. "The potential of growing dependence rather than interdependence
2. The loss of employment opportunities
3. An addition to balance-of-payments problems
4. The danger of loss of legitimate access to vital information
5. The danger that industrial and social development will largely be governed by decisions of interest groups residing in other countries"

As might be expected from a conference whose participants represented a wide range of interests—"stake-holders" as they are called in the address—there was no simple consensus on the issues raised. It is clear, and this appears in the remarks of the panelists as well as the summary of views of the rapporteurs, that the centre of balance of opinion at the conference was considerably less alarmist than the minister's five-point warning.

Computer industry participants, who were in the majority, were far more concerned about the possible *negative* effects on them (and on various aspects of the Canadian economy) that might come from misguided government regulation than they were about any trend in job losses (actual or potential). In the words of George Fierheller, the most articulate spokesman of this point of view, protection of domestic computer services might become counter-productive. He saw a real danger that Canadian policy makers might inadvertantly and prematurely freeze the technology. Even those who felt that the data flow question of greatest importance was the *qualitative* issue—the data transmission associated with planning, design, and control of enterprises being the most vital—were concerned that protective measures would raise the cost of doing business in Canada, and in the absence of a better business environment, result in more harm than good.

One workshop agreed with Dr. Peter Robinson that there is a potential problem of absolute job loss resulting from trends in transborder data flows, but professed not to know how great the loss would be; another group thought that there was no problem; a third "somewhat agreed that we need to ascertain the volume," but went on to observe that the definition of the problems arising from transborder data flows was far from clear. Those who minimized the job loss problem tended to stress that the real difficulties facing Canada would not be job loss but rather inadequate supply of trained people to match the demand.

Everyone appeared certain that the problems addressed at the conference are multidimensional, that they are not susceptible to global solution, and that great care must be taken by governments to assure that—if action is taken in the name of protecting against job losses, privacy, or whatever—the international development of computer communications technology not be inhibited. For those who admitted the necessity or inevitability of government intervention, serious concern was expressed over "ad hockery": several spokesmen commented on the apparent lack of any underlying federal government policy concerning the regulation of transborder data flows. One rapporteur noted that his group reached the conclusion, "albeit with a bit of dilemma," that the government of Canada requires an information infrastructure strategy, one that would "emphasize the positive in removing impediments, and so on, through looking at opportunities and de-emphasizing the problems."

Perhaps the best summary was not delivered at the conference at all, but rather appeared in a letter which we received a few days later from one of the participants, Gaston Beauséjour from the ministère des Communications, Québec, who wanted to expand upon a point of view which he had expressed in public:

> Such an expenditure [for this conference] will have been a very small and worthwhile INVESTMENT if we have grown a little wiser, and if this dialogue is to be followed by a number of positive actions and by future discussions towards the resolution of the issues raised.
>
> However, it will have been a sad WASTE of time, effort and money if, tomorrow, we all remain more or less with the same opinions and perceptions as we had when we first came to the conference.
>
> To be more precise and candid: it will have been a sad waste if we, Canadians, do not attempt to rid ourselves of some of the paralysing FEARS which are so often typical of importing nations. And it will have been a sad waste if our friendly neighbours do not attempt, in realistic terms, to reduce and control the overwhelming GREED which is often typical of exporting nations.
>
> In the French culture, we do not speak of "tigers,"* but we do have a fable about "the chicken that lays golden eggs," which is pertinent in this matter, I think.
>
> Indeed, I trust that it has been made abundantly clear by most of the Canadians who were attending the Conference that they hope the Canadian Government(s) will not kill the chicken by opening-up its intestines in an attempt to regulate and control its ability to lay the golden eggs (as the poor soul did in the French fable).
>
> However, I hope that it has also been understood by our fellow Americans that we too, Canadians, want a piece of the action, want our share of the golden eggs. More importantly: that we too, Canadians, want to have an opportunity to breed a few generations of *chickens of our own* which have full ability to lay some of the golden eggs of the INFORMATION AGE.

---

* This was a reference to a remark made by Gordon B. Thompson, Bell Northern Research, during the audience response period: "It has been said that if you hunt rabbits and tigers you have to keep your eye out for tigers. However, if you hunt tigers, you do not have to keep your eye out for rabbits. I would suggest that what I have been hearing this morning is a bunch of rabbit hunters in tiger country, but unfortunately, the tigers are yet to be born."

Introduction

par
David Hoffman
Institut de recherches politiques

La conférence-atelier dont l'Institut de recherches politiques publie maintenant le compte rendu tire son origine d'un projet de recherche établi dans le cadre du Programme d'études de prospective. Zavis P. Zeman, directeur du projet et, à ce titre, responsable d'une série d'analyses portant sur l'impact futur des changements technologiques et économiques sur le Canada, Bill Cundiff, premier adjoint à la recherche, et Robert Russel, alors rédacteur-conseil du programme, ont abordé le sujet à partir d'un cadre relativement simple. Ils devaient identifier les progrès technologiques visant à faciliter la circulation outre-frontières des données informatiques et soupeser les conséquences sociales et surtout économiques sur le Canada du maintien ou même de l'accélération de ces tendances. Le point principal, tel qu'il apparaît dans le document de travail de Bill Cundiff, n'est pas tant la circulation des données que l'exode hors des frontières des travaux liés au traitement de ces données. Pour être plus précis—le sens prévisible de la circulation des données étant nord-sud et non l'inverse—il restait à déterminer quelle pouvait être l'incidence de la perte d'emplois et de la diminution des emplois disponibles au Canada.

Il était relativement facile de décrire les innovations technologiques, mais plus difficile d'en évaluer les conséquences économiques—même passées, sans parler des hypothèses ayant trait aux développements futurs. Nous avions à notre disposition l'excellent travail effectué dans ce domaine par l'ancien Secrétariat de la téléinformatique du ministère fédéral des Communications. Cependant, l'examen attentif des données nous révélait bientôt que les études qui sous-tendaient l'analyse étaient tirées d'un échantillon tellement restreint qu'il devenait impossible d'en déduire des tendances à long terme. Les données des séries chronologiques, en particulier, présentaient des fluctuations cycliques qui gênaient le tracé des courbes. Par conséquent, toute projection à long terme aurait été risquée. Néanmoins, nous avions suffisamment de preuves qu'il fallait tenir compte de ces questions.

L'une des conclusions du travail de recherche—pour laquelle nous espérions vraiment recevoir l'accord des participants à la conférence—fut la nécessité d'une étude plus approfondie que toutes celles réalisées jusqu'à maintenant afin d'établir les faits; une étude portant sur les travaux informatiques des principales sociétés canadiennes était impérative si l'on voulait obtenir les données indispensables à l'analyse des politiques et l'établissement ultérieur de politiques. Les lecteurs de ce compte rendu pourront constater que seule une minorité des participants à la conférence nous a accordé son appui.

La perspective première de l'étude de Bill Cundiff était orientée sur la technologie. En d'autres mots, on a considéré que l'expansion rapide de la téléinformatique, que facilitent des innovations telles la commutation par paquets, les satellites et le raccordement des réseaux de télécommunication installés aux Etats-Unis au réseau Datapac de Bell Canada, avait un impact du fait que les données transmises pouvaient difficilement être soumises à l'expédition douanière normale ou à tout autre contrôle. Cependant, à mesure que les recherches se poursuivaient, il devenait évident que la centralisation de la comptabilité, de la vérification et du traitement des données dans les sociétés mères américaines tenait peut-être moins au fait d'une nouvelle technologie économique et simplifiée, qu'à celui d'un style de gestion particulier. Cette centralisation découlait de la structure internationale des sociétés en question. Celles qui sont des "répliques miniatures", produisant un faible pourcentage seulement des produits de la société mère américaine, sont moins susceptibles de confier au siège social leurs principales activités informatiques. Cette analyse a renforcé le sentiment qu'une étude élaborée, qui tiendrait compte des variables structurelles, était nécessaire.

L'intérêt porté aux conséquences économiques plus qu'à la question du secret s'est avéré un facteur déterminant dans la décision ultérieure d'utiliser les résultats de ces recherches comme fondement de l'organisation d'une conférence internationale. La franchise évidente, manifestée par une attaque directe du point le plus important, a retenu l'attention des deux côtés de la frontière, et Bill Cundiff est revenu de la *1978 National Computer Conference,* tenue à Anaheim, Californie, sous les auspices de l'*American Federation of Information Processing Societies* (AFIPS), persuadé que le problème était mûr pour la discussion. Les événements eurent tôt fait de lui donner raison. Comme le disait l'un des participants à la conférence, Oswald Ganley de l'université Harvard: "Il s'agit de . . . la première réunion où tombe enfin le voile du secret qui recouvrait ces discussions depuis deux ans et où nous acceptons enfin le fait que les questions abordées sont en réalité des questions culturelles et économiques importantes.''

Un comité d'experts a été formé afin d'offrir aux participants un large éventail de perspectives; en voici les membres.
— Morris Crawford, directeur intérimaire, Office of Bilateral and Multilateral Science and Technology Programs, U.S. Department of State, Washington
— John M. Eger, avocat, Washington
— George Fierheller, président, Systems Dimensions Ltée, Ottawa
— J.C. Grant, directeur général adjoint, Systems Development, Banque Royale du Canada, Montréal
— A.M. McMahon, vice-président, Communications informatiques, Bell Canada, Ottawa
— Brendan McShane, spécialiste-conseil en services informatiques, Bethesda
— Peter Robinson, conseiller en politique, ministère des Communications, téléinformatique, Ottawa

Chacun des membres du comité était invité à préparer à l'avance un bref ensemble de commentaires sur la question de la circulation des données outre-frontières. Ces commentaires ont été réunis et envoyés, accompagnés d'un exemplaire du document de travail, à toutes les personnes inscrites à la conférence. Ainsi les participants pouvaient-ils travailler à partir du point de vue officiel du comité et du rapport de recherche de l'Institut qui servirait de base à la principale allocution de Bill Cundiff. Comme prévu, cette façon de procéder a vite entraîné une confrontation des principales questions, car, à la suite de l'allocution, les membres du comité passèrent immédiatement à la critique mutuelle de leurs positions antérieures respectives.

Au cours de l'après-midi, les quelque soixante participants se sont partagés en quatre ateliers, présidés par les membres du comité; ces derniers devaient en outre jouer le rôle de rapporteurs. Les discussions devaient cerner cinq zones de danger potentiel reliées aux communications informatiques transnationales, dangers qu'avait identifiés, en été 1977, J. Hugh Faulkner, alors ministre d'Etat à la Science et à la Technologie. L'un des groupes, au dire du rapporteur, "a élargi le sujet et discuté ouvertement, sans contrainte", ne respectant donc pas le plan prévu; mais les trois autres groupes ont essayé de se concentrer sur les thèmes suivants:

1. "La possibilité d'une dépendance croissante plutôt que d'une interdépendance
2. La perte de certaines possibilités d'emploi
3. Des problèmes accrus au niveau de la balance des paiements
4. Le danger d'une perte de l'accès légitime aux informations vitales
5. Le danger que le développement industriel et social soit assujetti aux décisions prises par des groupes d'intérêts d'autres pays"

Il était à prévoir, dans une conférence dont les participants représentent une vaste gamme d'intérêts—qualifiés dans l'allocution de "personnes détenant les enjeux"—qu'il n'y aurait pas consensus facile sur les questions abordées. Cependant, il paraît évident, suivant les remarques posées par les membres du comité et la synthèse des points de vue préparée par les rapporteurs, qu'au total, les opinions émises lors de la conférence étaient beaucoup moins alarmistes que ne le laissait entendre l'avertissement formulé en cinq points par le ministre.

Les participants issus de l'industrie de l'informatique, constituant la majorité, se préoccupaient bien davantage des effets *négatifs* que pourrait avoir sur eux (et sur certains éléments de l'économie canadienne) une réglementation gouvernementale malencontreuse, que de toute tendance à la perte d'emplois (réelle ou potentielle). Comme l'a déclaré George Fierheller, défenseur le plus convaincu de ce point de vue, la protection des services d'ordinateurs domestiques pourrait s'avérer contre-productrice. Il craint véritablement que les Canadiens chargés de l'élaboration de politiques puissent, par inadvertance et de façon prématurée, geler la technologie. Même ceux qui pensaient que la question la plus importante liée à la circulation des données se situait au niveau *qualitatif*—la transmission des données associée à la planification, à la création et au contrôle des entreprises étant primordiale—craignaient que les mesures de protection n'augmentent le coût des affaires traitées au Canada et, qu'en l'absence d'un environnement commercial plus propice, il ne résulte plus de mal que de bien.

L'un des ateliers, à l'instar de M. Peter Robinson, a jugé qu'il existait un problème latent de perte absolue d'emplois découlant de ces tendances de la circulation des données outre-frontières, mais a déclaré ne pas connaître l'importance de cette perte éventuelle. Un autre groupe a conclu qu'il n'existait aucun problème. Et un troisième s'est "en quelque sorte entendu sur la nécessité d'en mesurer l'ampleur", tout en observant que la définition des problèmes causés par la circulation des données outre-frontières n'était pas du tout claire. Ceux qui minimisaient le problème de la perte d'emplois insistaient sur le fait que les difficultés réelles auxquelles le Canada serait exposé ne seraient pas celles de la perte d'emplois, mais plutôt celles d'une insuffisance de personnel compétent pour répondre à la demande.

Tous étaient persuadés que les problèmes soulevés lors de la conférence recelaient plusieurs dimensions, qu'ils ne pouvaient faire l'objet d'une solution globale et que les gouvernements devaient prendre grand soin—si des mesures devaient être prises en vue de se protéger de la perte d'emplois, à l'égard du secret, ou quoi que ce soit d'autre—de ne pas freiner le développement international de la technologie de la téléinformatique. Ceux qui ont admis la nécessité ou le caractère inévitable d'une intervention gouvernementale ont soulevé la question de "l'opportunité": plusieurs porte-parole ont souligné l'absence apparente de toute politique gouvernementale fédérale de base concernant la réglementation de la circulation des données outre-frontières. Un rapporteur a noté que son groupe en est arrivé à la conclusion, "non sans quelque remous", que le gouvernement du Canada requiert une stratégie d'infrastructure de l'information qui "insisterait sur le côté positif de l'abolition des obstacles, et ainsi de suite, et sur les possibilités plutôt que sur les problèmes".

Peut-être la meilleure synthèse n'a-t-elle pas été donnée lors de la conférence elle-même, mais dans une lettre que nous faisait parvenir quelques jours plus tard l'un des participants, Gaston Beauséjour, du ministère des Communications du Québec, reprenant l'argument qu'il avait exposé en public:

> De telles dépenses [pour cette conférence] représentent un bien maigre et précieux INVESTISSEMENT si elles nous ont assagis et si ces entretiens sont suivis d'un certain nombre d'initiatives positives et d'autres discussions visant à répondre aux questions soulevées.
>
> Toutefois, elles n'auront été qu'une triste PERTE de temps, d'efforts et d'argent si, demain, nous nous retrouvons tous plus ou moins avec les mêmes idées et la même façon de voir les choses qu'avant cette conférence.
>
> Pour être plus précis et plus franc, elles auront malheureusement été vaines si nous, Canadiens, n'essayons pas de nous libérer de certaines des CRAINTES paralysantes si souvent typiques des nations importatrices. Et vaines également si nos voisins et amis n'essaient pas, dans la réalité, de réduire et de contrôler l'irrésistible CUPIDITÉ qui, souvent, est l'apanage des nations exportatrices.

Dans la culture française, nous ne parlons pas de "tigres"*; mais nous avons une fable sur "la poule aux oeufs d'or" qui, je pense, s'applique bien au cas présent.

Je crois, en réalité, que la plupart des Canadiens qui ont assisté à cette conférence ont établi très clairement qu'ils souhaitent que le(s) gouvernement(s) canadien(s) ne tuera(ont) pas la poule en lui ouvrant le ventre à dessein d'en régler et d'en contrôler la ponte d'oeufs d'or (comme l'a fait ce pauvre homme de la fable française).

J'espère cependant que nos amis américains ont compris que nous aussi, Canadiens, voulons notre part des oeufs d'or. Et plus important encore, que nous aussi, Canadiens, voulons avoir la possibilité d'élever quelques générations de *poules bien à nous,* qui pourront bel et bien pondre quelques-uns des oeufs d'or de l'ÈRE DE L'INFORMATION.

---

* Le terme se rapporte à une remarque faite par Gordon B. Thompson, de *Bell Northern Research,* au cours de la période de questions: "Lorsqu'on chasse les lapins et les tigres, dit-on, c'est à l'affût des tigres qu'il faut rester. Mais lorsqu'on chasse le tigre, point n'est besoin d'épier le lapin. Or, il ressort de ce que nous avons entendu ce matin qu'il s'agit d'un groupe de chasseurs de lapins dans un pays où le tigre est roi; mais malheureusement, les tigres ne sont pas encore nés."

Chapter One

Issues in Canadian/U.S. Transborder Computer Data Flows

by
W.E. Cundiff
Institute for Research on Public Policy

Several events and trends of the 1970s signal the beginning of a long international battle involving governments and the buyers and sellers of computer and communications technology. The battle, which will likely continue well into the 1980s, is over the erosion of national borders and the effect this has on the loci of power in society. Whether the reasons given are for the protection of cultural values, personal privacy,[1] technological advancement, or national sovereignty, the encompassing theme is the preservation or enhancement of the power to control and direct operations in the best interest of the nation-state.

Perceived erosion of national borders and resulting alarm in many nations is caused by the rapid expansion of computer communications, which operate in such a way that the transmission of data cannot be easily made subject to normal clearance by customs or other controls. As it stands now, one may access a computer network from virtually anywhere without anyone else knowing the nature of the transactions carried out while on-line with a computer. Because of this, computer users, including the richest business interests, will increasingly be able to choose where they want to live, and store information where they wish. As computer communications become a key factor in the operations of multinational corporations, governmental policy makers may find it increasingly difficult to regulate effectively in areas of international commerce.

A great deal of concern is at present focused on the implications of the flow of computer data across national boundaries. Questions regarding the protection of personal privacy and national sovereignty are the impetus for a number of government efforts around the world aimed at formulating policies. Actions

---

[1] While often mentioned in the context of transnational data regulation, the computer privacy issues will not be covered here owing to their thorough treatment by several others and their less central importance in the theme developed here (e.g., the Rand Corporation alone offers over fifty research documents on "Privacy and the Computer Age").

taken by nations to control transborder data flows may have international economic ramifications. Such measures have even been likened by some to protectionism in international trade. Others identify the computer network as a future market-place, and see computer data as a vital commodity as important to the nation's economic health as physical goods.[2]

The broad dimensions of potential social crisis, brought about through the application of transnational computer communications, were outlined by the former Canadian minister of state for Science and Technology, J. Hugh Faulkner, in a Toronto speech in August 1977. In his official opening address to the 1977 Congress of the International Federation for Information Processing meeting in Toronto, he spoke of how advances in computer communications have acted to "accentuate the problem of national control over national destinies." He went on to discuss the potential for altering organizational structure in order to gain increased control for corporations, and how this may have "worrisome implications for Canada and many other countries." Continuing, Mr. Faulkner said: "The export of information processing capacity results in the loss of jobs and the erosion of job opportunities in a high technology area." He likened such a migration of computing power to the post-war brain drain of the forties and fifties, and then outlined five areas of potential danger thus created:

1. "The potential of growing dependence rather than interdependence
2. The loss of employment opportunities
3. An addition to balance-of-payments problems
4. The danger of loss of legitimate access to vital information
5. The danger that industrial and social development will largely be governed by the decisions of interest groups residing in another country"

The five areas of impact described here span many levels of society. The stake-holders are numerous and the impacts represent a potential threat to national, social, and economic stability. Because of this, sufficient attention must be given to developing an accurate appraisal of the dynamics of Canadian/U.S. transborder computing as soon as possible. As will be shown later, the pace of developments in transnational data regulation is moving very quickly, and it is possible that policy makers may feel an urgency to act in the absence of a complete analysis. As a first step toward providing the needed information for decision making, this paper highlights the issues surrounding Canadian/U.S. transborder computer data flows and establishes a rationale for comprehensive analysis.

---

[2] This is the view of Gordon Thompson in "The Information Market-Place" being prepared for publication by the Institute for Research on Public Policy.

THE STAKE-HOLDERS

The vested interests are principally in five areas:
1. governments
2. communications carriers
3. computer manufacturers
4. multinational companies
5. service bureaux

The governmental stake-holders are numerous and are especially concerned because of the implications for tax legislation, industrial development, general foreign trade, and employment. Federal government departments figuring strongly in this include Finance; Industry, Trade and Commerce; Communications; and Employment and Immigration. While these four can be seen as the main initiators of action, other government departments, such as Justice and External Affairs, are important in deriving solutions through their "draftsman" and adviser roles.

The communications carriers are in the business of providing the "highways," and as far as they are concerned, the more data traffic the better—whether it is a North-South or East-West flow. The carriers involved provide both private leased-line services and public networks for connecting people and computers. The key interests include Bell and CNCP in Canada, while A.T.&T. and extensions such as the "value-added" Telenet and Tymnet networks figure strongly on the U.S. side.

Computer manufacturers, particularly the large standard-bearers, such as IBM, Digital Equipment Corporation (DEC), and Control Data Corporation (CDC), are committing a very significant marketing thrust toward network-oriented products. This involves the development of elaborate software and hardware, including satellites for linking computers and terminals in a unified network architecture. It should be noted that in some cases the strategy of a manufacturer is also to offer services through the network.

Major multinational companies increasingly rely on computer communications as a form of "nervous system" for the co-ordination of functions in the corporate body. While in many cases actual carrier-supplied lines are not used to move data between branch and head offices, data are nevertheless physically transported for processing. Whether by electronics or by other means, the uninterrupted movement of corporate data and the freedom to process data where it best serves the company are of key importance to corporate performance. In the context of Canadian/U.S. transnational computing, this important free flow probably applies to all companies operating in both countries.

The domestic and international data services industry, of course, has a strong vested interest, as its vitality depends on the action of government, the carriers, and manufacturers and client companies. As such, the service bureaux are arguably the most sensitive to the issues surrounding Canadian/U.S. transborder data flows. It is not solely the concern of those companies which operate internationally and require open access to foreign markets. Even the small community data processing businesses are subject to competition from computers located in foreign countries.

There are many other groups which could be said to have vested interests in these issues. The Canadian Radio-television and Telecommunications Commission (CRTC) is involved in deliberating the regulatory measures in computer communications. The TransCanada Telephone System, an association of major provincial telephone companies and the Telesat domestic satellite system, co-ordinates national systems and service planning, and administers Canadian/U.S. revenue distribution between member companies. Many provincial authorities are also concerned in a more indirect, yet significant, way. Attention in Quebec, for instance, is directed at the extent to which the local computer services industry is subject to domination by outside forces—a perspective which evolved through interprovincial considerations. Educational and research institutions increasingly rely on computerized data bases, which are accessible only through international networks. The free flow of this information is increasingly vital to scientific and technological progress.

THE TECHNOLOGICAL TREND

The convergence of computers and communications, abetted by advancements in packet switching and satellite technologies, is forecast to cause great social change in the coming decade. It has been widely suggested that information processing, by way of computer communications, will increasingly become the key principal activity of most people in a post-industrial society. If one takes notice of the advances in computer communications which have already occurred, as well as the forecasts of what is likely to occur over the next decade or so, two things are evident. Notably, the cost of computing has declined rapidly as has the cost of communicating computer data. Because of technological advances, the users of computers are increasingly able to tailor the available computing power to specific needs and style. The distance between user and machine becomes much less a factor in planning the ideal data processing environment. With the advent of smaller, yet powerful, computers which are able to "talk" to the big computers, data processing can be geographically distributed via a common network. New networks are being constructed, and "distributed processing" is still a buzz phrase in the computing industry in spite of many who have viewed it as a passing fad. Some computer manufacturers are staking their future on the ability to interconnect the computers they sell by vast networks of satellites and land lines. Multinational corporations look forward to what the new computer communications will do for their balance sheet, as they hope to expand and refine their range of control farther and farther.

Packet switching

One of the advances which is already affecting the trend in computer communications involves breaking data into standardized "packets," which are then sent along the most optimal route to be reassembled at the receiving end. Whereas conventional circuit switching sent a complete message along a single link connecting sender and receiver, packet switching relies on the use of many channels selected according to their availability at a particular instant. Because these channels can be used by multiple users, it is possible, in effect, to spread the associated costs among the users, and create a rate structure based mainly on the amount of data sent rather than the amount of leased bandwidth or connect time.

The rates for packet switching versus circuit switching are much less sensitive to distance. This can result in dramatic rate reductions such as I.P. Sharp Associates' recent drop from eight dollars per hour to one dollar per hour for connect time. Part of the I.P. Sharp strategy was also to increase the price of character transmission. It can be seen that packet switching can have strong consequences depending on the type of application being processed. For example, the fairly regular communication of large blocks of data may be costly by packet switching—even at short distances. On the other hand, sending and receiving more modest amounts of data even thousands of miles can be much less expensive than before.

Satellites

Even more outstanding is the potential that satellites hold for computer communications. Today, satellite communications require leasing a set of individual channels to accommodate various kinds of data from voice, video, and computer services. New technology will enable transmission via a single channel and allow for a more substantial use of available capacity at lower costs.

In the forefront of commercial development of satellites is Satellite Business Systems (SBS), which is a consortium of IBM, COMSAT General Corporation, and Aetna Life & Casualty Company. The SBS service will rely on small earth stations, installed on a customer's premises, that will enable sending data among remote corporate locations hundreds of times faster than before. It has been speculated that by boosting the range and timeliness of corporate information through satellite communications, basic changes will occur in the way business is conducted. According to an SBS spokesman, the effect of integrating widely dispersed corporate communications will be like that of the private branch exchange (PBX) inside a single office. A trend may be toward increased interest in centralized computing in geographically dispersed organizations.[3] Large

---

[3] This outlook was presented by Ronald W. McCabe, a representative of Satellite Business Systems, at the American Federation of Information Processing Societies' (AFIPS) 1978 National Computer Conference in Anaheim, California, June 5-8, 1978.

corporate data bases could be maintained centrally, with the capability to distribute part or all to branch operations by way of high rate communications between computers. Because of their capacity for integrating all known types of electronic media within one central complex, those who command the satellites may also command societal information in the near future.[4]

A continental net

On May 3, 1978, interim approval of tariffs was granted by the CRTC linking the American-based networks of Telenet Communications Corporation and Tymshare Inc. with Bell Canada's Datapac network. All three networks utilize what is known as the X.25 protocol standard, which makes it relatively easy to interconnect different networks. The overall effect is to produce a continental network where the computing resources of each country are much more easily accessible and affordable from any location.

The further development of the networks in the United States will link them to other networks in Europe and elsewhere around the world. It may be that the United States will expand its role as an intermediate link in the communications chain between Canada and other countries. At present, many American branch offices of Japanese, European, and other foreign companies have well-established computer communications to their head offices half-way around the world. Rather than establish communications lines between Canada and these far remote points, Canadian subsidiaries merely tie-in across the border to the existing network for their corporate data transactions. This sort of activity is frustrating to a Canadian organization like Teleglobe in its attempts to build an international gateway, and market international telecommunications directly between Canada and foreign centres.

Many communications carriers are gearing up for what will be a very rich market. A great deal of planning is going into determining the potential number of lines, the topology of the networks, the amount of bandwidth, and other technical factors. The technical and logistical problems associated with broadening computer communications are vast, and on top of this, regulatory problems are apparent in ever-increasing magnitude because of technological advancements. One need only cite the current battle between A.T.&T. and IBM in the U.S. Federal Communications Commission, where the problem is essentially one of deciding where communications become computing in networks. The increasing incorporation of microprocessor technology into networks has compounded this thorny issue which may take years to solve. It is generally agreed that the global communications revolution forecast by such prestigious research groups as Arthur D. Little Inc. may be slowed down by such disputes, and in particular because of the current concern for transborder regulations.[5]

---

[4] Pierre Kohler, *Les satellites: maîtres du monde* (Paris: Hachette, 1978).
[5] G. Russell Pipe, "The Day of the Data Barrier," *Computing Europe*, February 2, 1978, pp. 15-16.

INTERNATIONAL ACTION

Response to potential problems created by the changing technology is wide-spread, with a number of intergovernmental organizations working toward the development of policy guide-lines for transnational data flows.[6] Back in 1973, the European Economic Community (EEC) made statements in a commission report calling for the establishment of common measures concerning individual rights and computer-based information systems. Subsequent attention has been directed toward studying various items of legislation of the member states in order to determine the need for an EEC directive on data bank protection. Since 1975, the Nordic Council has concentrated on "harmonizing" the privacy laws among the four member countries. The approach is to avoid having to develop a complicated international agreement by assuring that individual member laws complement each other. Concern within the Council of Europe extends back to 1971 when a committee was established to study the requirement for privacy protection in computer-based information systems. Work continued toward achieving increased co-operation among the nineteen members and a new committee was established in 1976, aimed at identifying the problems associated with transnational data flows. The twenty-four-member Organisation for Economic Co-operation and Development (OECD) has sponsored research on transnational data flows. The OECD Data Bank Panel has investigated technological, economic, social, and legal aspects, and in September 1977, an international symposium was held in Vienna to further its work. A successor to the Data Bank Panel, the Expert Group on Transborder Data Barriers and the Protection of Privacy, met for the first time in the spring of 1978, and is scheduled for a full group meeting in December 1978.

Work is also under way in countries such as the United Kingdom to determine more equitable tariffs on the transborder shipment of information contained in computer media. At present, charges are levied on the cost of the media (e.g., punched cards, magnetic tape, or disk) rather than the actual software or data. What is occurring, in effect, is the movement of multi-thousand-dollar software across boundaries as though its worth amounted to thirty dollars: the cost of a 2400-foot reel of magnetic computer tape! It is proving to be a difficult issue to resolve. If the practice of non-computer-mediated transmission of data under the coverage of data protection laws were to be entirely curtailed, then a wholesale inspection of parcels for contraband data would have to come into effect.

In many of the publications addressing the problems of transnational data regulation, Canada is mentioned as one of the participants in the data protection movement. For some time, Canadians have been concerned about the amount of

---

[6] A good source document on the legislation in several countries is *Selected Foreign National Data Protection Laws and Bills*, U.S., Department of Commerce, edited by Charles Wilk. Also, for an on-going account of the issues in data flow legislation, see *Transnational Data Report*, published eight times a year by the Wayne Smith Company, Washington, D.C.

U.S. information which flows into Canada by way of print and electronic media. On the other hand, Canadians are also concerned about what flows out of Canada in the form of data for processing on U.S. computers. According to a restricted federal document on Canadian/U.S. information flows, there exist no fewer than ninety-two provincial and twenty-three federal pieces of legislation which could be applied to transborder handling and storage of data.[7] Many are oriented to specific industries such as insurance, mining, and banking, while others are more general and deal for instance with customs, business incorporation, and taxation. For most, the key stipulation is that data on certain operations must be kept in Canada.

While legislation affecting the transnational flow of computer data is at various stages of development in several countries, Sweden, the best known example, has operated its Data Inspection Board since 1974. Data banks containing information about the activities of individual citizens may not be constructed without permission of the "Inspectorate." If any personal information is intended for use outside Sweden, its issuance also depends on special permission.

Although the erecting of data barriers along the lines of the Swedish example is usually done in the name of protecting personal privacy, it is becoming clear that other central forces are at work. Some nations are intent on protecting or building expertise in information products and services in order to secure their participation in the growing knowledge industry. The effect is to expand employment opportunities in a new sector and provide for growth in the national economy.[8]

For whatever reason, the trend appears to be toward increased data regulation, particularly in Europe. While this may be an expanding problem between nations, contrasting trends do appear within nations, as exemplified by the on-going U.S. debate on the deregulation of all communications.

THE CORPORATE CONCERN

Multinational companies are beginning to show concern about the interference in corporate communications that could result from data protection laws. Until recently, companies have enjoyed little interference in sending corporate records back and forth between offices in different countries. It is now feared that if, for instance, limitations are imposed on where personnel records containing information on individuals can be stored, then other forms of data may also become subject to regulation. Limitations on how marketing, planning, or financial data are handled could upset a company's international operations,

---

[7] These are listed in the Department of Communications, Computer/Communications Secretariat report, *North/South Flow of Information: Jurisdictional Considerations,* September 1976.

[8] For an industry-oriented view of this point and the general issues surrounding transnational data regulation see Angeline Pantages and G. Russell Pipe, "A New Headache of International DP," *Datamation,* June 1977, pp. 115-23.

especially if such limitations required data to be processed or stored only in the country of origin. While the advances in computer communications may widen the spectrum of control of multinational corporations, the present uncertainty is most surely having a confusing effect on many operations. Corporate planners, at least for those countries most advanced in data protection laws, are having to take a second look at their strategic plans for implementing new computer installations and telecommunications linkages with branch operations. To further complicate the situation, when setting up data barriers for national self-interest, countries act to thwart the successful establishment of world-wide standards for computer network interface and access protocols. Changes in rate structure for communications lines can have serious consequences. Depending on the type of application, a switch from a fixed-rate, leased line to a rate based on the volume of data transmitted over the line could add greatly to the costs of communicating computer data. This economic impetus has already appeared in Italy, where before the Consultative Committee on International Telephone and Telegraph (CCITT) a proposal for a volume-sensitive rate structure to replace fixed-rate leasing is gaining ground. The initiation of this new pricing scheme would increase profits for Italy, but would be a severe irritant to multinational companies operating there.

An international gap

Many corporate officers who should be aware of developments in transnational data regulation do not know what actions have been, or are about to be, taken in their own countries and elsewhere: that is to say, laws are being enacted which dictate what type of data may be stored and where they may be legally stored. In a mid-1977 survey on transnational data flows conducted by *Datamation,* and directed to *Fortune's* top 1000 U.S. companies, only forty responses were received. The reaction of most was that they did not know about the issues being probed and that it was probably not important that they do know.[9] Concern has since begun to grow in the business community though. At the On-line Conference on Transnational Data Regulation held in Brussels in early February 1978, the concerted voice of business was heard. Over one hundred American businessmen presented their cases to the European contingent that the free flow of computer communications must exist and will benefit all. It has been suggested that finally, through data barrier legislation, the Europeans have found a way to "blunt" American technological dominance. Multinational corporations may be beginning to understand that they have much to lose, as do the dominant American computer manufacturers and data servicers.

---

[9] A short summary of this survey appears in Angeline Pantages, "Is The World Building Data Barriers?" *Datamation,* December 1977, pp. 90-98.

CANADIAN/U.S. TRANSBORDER FLOW: CURRENT RESEARCH ACTIVITY

It has been noted recently that it has been impossible for A.T.&.T. to quantify the magnitude of data moving across the Canadian/U.S. border. It has also been noted that the number of private lines is about equal to the number for public access, and it may be impossible to know more about the nature of the data transmitted without corporate co-operation.[10] At present, very little knowledge has been accumulated regarding the transborder flow between Canada and the United States. In preparing this working paper, approximately forty experts in computer communications in Canada and the United States were consulted. The purpose was to assess the extent to which research has been directed at Canadian/U.S. data flows, and to better determine if there exist potential problems which require study. The discussions indicated virtually no work in this area, either past or on-going. Many individuals did, however, see the potential for problems of job loss, further imbalance of payments, and erosion of national autonomy. The response of many, particularly Americans, was that if any problems are likely to appear, except for those normally associated with market planning, then they will probably be Canada's problems.

Datamation

In the earlier mentioned *Datamation* survey on transnational data flows, twenty of the forty respondents had data processing operations in Canada.[11] Because some did not give specific answers to all questions, the actual number is most likely greater. Six out of the twenty stated that they use no on-line links between branches and American head offices. Twelve have on-line links between Canadian branches and American head offices, including interactive terminals and remote job entry. A few have computer-to-computer links. Some of the Canadian sites are autonomous, with on-line services available from the head office for specialized applications or when a larger machine is required. In certain cases, much of the data flow between Canada and the United States is by mail or telex, and tapes are sent back and forth in some instances.

The type of data sent over boundaries varies, with financial and marketing data leading the list, followed by production/distribution and personnel data. In many cases, summary reports are used, but for the five of seventeen firms which send personnel records, quite detailed information is transmitted. One insurance company noted that its customer data are transmitted across the border to a U.S. computer. The company is worried about possible prohibitions being placed on

---

[10] A.T.&.T., at the request of William H. Read of the Harvard Program on Information Resources Policy, attempted to determine the number and kinds of circuits between the two countries. See William H. Read, "Network Control in Global Communications," *Telecommunications Policy*, March 1977, pp. 135-37.

[11] Non-proprietary information regarding the results of the survey was communicated informally to the author by the principal investigator.

this activity since it would cost a fortune to establish a computer installation in Canada large enough to handle the Canadian processing now done in the United States. A few firms said they are tracking Canadian action in this area because of the impacts such limitations might have on current operations. One representative said that his firm is planning to tie together several hundred Canadian locations on-line to a central American computer centre. However, he did allow: "But we may have to maintain a Canadian data centre at significantly higher cost."

Professor Baar's study

A preliminary analysis of relations between head offices and branches was conducted recently by Professor Ellen Baar of York University.[12] The 200 largest industrial corporations in Canada, taken from the annual *Financial Post* listing, formed the basis of her sample. From this, 6 corporations were randomly drawn from 4 consecutive groups of 50, ordered from the largest to the smallest. The selection process resulted in only 14 of the 24 corporations drawn being American. One third of the companies stated that the computer was the most valuable means for corporate communications. The survey indicated, however, that the organization of computer functions in most companies is in considerable flux.

Trends toward centralized and decentralized computing were both noted. Four of the American-owned companies have foreign computer communications links. Two sorts of companies appear to use these links: marginal branches and comparatively small operations which are only beginning to acquire some autonomy in Canada. The latter are "miniature replicas," involved in the production of only a small segment of all of the products of the American parent firm. The marginal branches, however, maintain sole responsibility for producing one complete product line. Their production is aimed at a global market as opposed to a domestic market. These companies are without the authority to develop new product lines.

Marginal branches do not require much communication among themselves. Computer communications are used to transmit orders and monitor production from head offices to the different marginal branches. The size of the marginal branch determines whether there is a direct communications link to head office. Professor Baar suggests that the migration of computing power may be most likely to affect the marginal branch, which is often quite large, rather than smaller corporations having limited managerial functions in Canada.

---

[12] The preliminary information outlined here was communicated informally to the author by Professor Baar.

Computer/Communications Secretariat

The leading edge of research on Canadian/U.S. transborder computer data flows is in the work of the now disbanded Computer/Communications Secretariat (C/CS) of the federal Department of Communications (DOC).[13] It is largely through its efforts that concern over potential problems has become sufficiently elevated to promote meaningful discussion.

In 1977, the C/CS conducted a series of telephone surveys in order to gain a better understanding of the possible migration of computer use to the United States. A number of questions were put to several different populations of computer users. Some of the resulting statistics were as follows: out of 354 computer users, 45 used foreign computers to some extent and 34 of these were subsidiaries which used the parent computer. Approximately one half who used foreign computers also had Canadian computer installations. Between 1970 and 1976, the number of users of foreign computers increased from 14 to 44. During the same period, those who used only foreign computers, with no Canadian computing at all, increased from 4 to 22. Foreign computer users showed a median staff size of 615 and median sales of $32.5 million, while Canadian-only users had a staff of 463 and sales of $22.5 million.

A mail survey was also conducted, in conjunction with the Canadian Association of Data Processing Service Organizations (CADAPSO), directed at member service bureaux and their perception of the possible migration of computing out of Canada. The survey cited seventeen specific instances of shift from Canadian- to American-based computing. Twenty-five of the thirty-six respondents believed that a major problem was brewing for Canada's future with the migration of computer services to the United States. Some of the respondents offered specific reasons why computing was going to U.S. companies. Foremost was the requirement to process on the parent computer. Also, the greater availability of specialized software and data bases, and the lower hardware cost (no duty or sales tax) were seen as key reasons for the popularity of U.S. processors.

Calculations performed using a model of the Canadian data processing industry indicate that the Canadian industry may be headed for problems. The model developed at the C/CS computes the value of variables, including the jobs lost and the value of computing services lost due to Canadian importation from the United States. Estimates derived from running the model for 1985 show a loss of approximately 23,500 jobs and an imported computing value of $1.5 billion, increasing the deficit on the balance of payments. The job-loss figure is mainly for jobs not created due to competition from imports. The estimates given here are, by the admission of C/CS officers, conservative; different assumptions yield far greater impacts.

---

[13] Among the several C/CS reports bearing on issues in Canadian computer communications, of particular importance here is *The Growth of Computer/Communications in Canada,* rev. draft (Ottawa: March 1978).

Info-Dyne

In a recent Info-Dyne market analysis of remote computing services in Canada, fifteen major vendors and forty users were studied to identify the special characteristics of Canadian remote computing.[14] Users who were interviewed strongly preferred "solid, well-established, Canadian" service firms. The implications drawn from the Info-Dyne analysis were that loyalty to Canadian data service companies is high, and that while many users continually study the offerings of others, a change to a new vendor is unlikely unless there is a very strong cost advantage. It was further noted that the typical Canadian businessman is willing to depend entirely on external computing sources and forego the prestige of owning his own computer. A trend was identified that large companies without on-site computing power are on the increase. The fact that Canada's data processing markets are located in a few compact centres is seen as a reinforcement of this tendency.

Because of the small emphasis on developing hardware, the Canadian industry is considered less skilled in product-technology planning and product-marketing management, although sales expertise is considered good. Perhaps the report's most telling observation on the industry was that "lack of aggressive new product development by remote computing services vendors, combined with the progressiveness of Canadian users, signals the probability of increased competition from U.S. vendors."

EMERGING POLICY ISSUES

While the relevant research to date does not provide a firm basis for policy, it does collectively point to a number of issues which must be considered. These issues go far beyond technological considerations and in many cases transcend an approach to understanding at the two-nation level. In some cases, the international dimension may be better understood by considering the ways in which problems of similar scale and complexity have been approached in other areas. It is safe to say that the results of research and the broad set of related issues demand intensive study in order to better equip those who will decide future directions in computer communications policy.

Computing and decision trade-offs

Large corporations will likely continue the trend toward buying up many smaller companies and situating the ultimate corporate power in fewer and fewer organizations. As this happens, the number of channels for reporting between all of the subsidiaries and the head office will likely increase dramatically. Distributing the computing by way of intelligent terminals and minicomputers

---

[14] *Remote Computing Services in Canada* (Minneapolis: Info-Dyne Inc., 1977).

among the branches allows the pre-processing of raw data to occur locally. This information is then telecommunicated to a head office computer for further processing, leading to directives back to the branches. This approach is particularly attractive to those corporations utilizing links that use a volume-sensitive rate structure. The point is that with increased corporate growth there also goes increased responsibility for co-ordinating many, often disparate, operations. Diversification at once involves both the recognition of new forces within the overall corporate structure and the need for enhanced control over the entire operation.

The central issue regarding the distribution of computing functions could be the proportionate growth in the weight given to branch versus head office processing. At present, the debate over what really is occurring is unfocused. The implications are that the decisions will be made differently, or at least the locus of decision making will be shaped by the particular computer communications environment. If the weight given to greater centralization of computing power increases faster than distribution as multinationals take over more and more companies, then the effect on Canada would likely be one of greater migration of computing to head offices.

However, the phenomenon cannot be viewed only bilaterally. If corporate growth entails the absorption of industry in other parts of the world, then plans to further centralize computing would likely be for the collective good—not on a country-to-country basis. Although this dimension is little considered in discussions of transnational data regulation, it is central to the overall issue of the migration of corporate computing power.

The domination of U.S. computers

Ever since the introduction of computers into society, Canada, along with other countries, has been dominated by American industry. The feeling may be that, while the hardware domination is inescapable, the software should be developed by Canadians. However, without action, this sector of the industry is also subject to impact and U.S. domination just like the hardware sector. The reasons for not allowing further domination in this area become clear when one sees the record for Canada in the development of computer hardware.

Canada's electronics industry is relatively strong in the communications sector which, including household reception equipment, accounts for over fifty thousand employees working in approximately two hundred and eighty plants. Shipments amounted to $1,677 million in 1976, with $453 million of goods destined for export. However, imports of computers alone accounted for $428 million of the 1976 electronics import total of $1,622 million. It is interesting to note the extent to which the U.S.-dominated computer hardware industry has grown in Canada—an industry almost totally dependent on imports, with minimal offsetting exports of finished computers. Between 1970 and 1975, the number of computer installations is estimated to have grown from 2,700 to 11,085.[15]

In the meantime, the situation seems to be little improved. There are Canadian computers designed and manufactured by fast growing companies such as Micro Computer Machines Inc., Geac Canada Ltd., and Consolidated Computer Inc. According to the most recent census of the Canadian Information Processing Society (CIPS), computer installations have risen 14.5 per cent for the year ended May 1, 1977. The actual figures indicate an increase from 5,937 the year before to 6,799. The CIPS estimates do not account for computers renting for less than one thousand dollars a month, and as such do not reflect a trend detected by many industry analysts—the proliferation of small microprocessor-based systems. But still, the small systems field is also dominated by the American entrepreneurs, and this is increasingly felt in Canada. Recent forecasts by R.W. Evans Research Corporation indicate that of a total thirty-two thousand computers expected to be installed by 1980, about 80 per cent would rent for less than two thousand dollars a month.

Suggestions are frequently heard that the foreign domination must stop, and that the kind of consumerism which supports the penetration of the Canadian market cannot go on forever. Production and consumption, it is said, will one day have to be reconciled, and it is therefore best to return now to greater self-sufficiency.[16] Such a move might result in the domestic production of some inferior and more costly items, but in the long run, Canadians would benefit, or so it is said. However, except in some specific applications areas, it is very unlikely that Canada could develop a large, viable computer hardware industry.[17] Rather than over-concern ourselves with the hardware side of computing, it may be wiser to focus on the fact that software is what makes a computer versatile, and it is people who give machines the capability to carry out complex operations. Canada has strong capabilities in writing software and it would seem necessary to further this expertise.

The network entrepreneur

Canadian remote computing service bureaux serve the Canadian-user community well with approximately one hundred and forty active firms. Nationalistic influence has been instrumental in shaping the hardware environment of this sector of the industry. While large companies such as Control Data

---

[15] These estimates were taken from *The Canadian Electronics Market* (Toronto: Maclean-Hunter, April 1977). Several sources of statistics on Canadian computer communications currently exist, and depending on the sampling approach, differ somewhat in their estimates.

[16] The importance of "technological sovereignty" has been widely stated by Josef Kates, chairman of the Science Council of Canada. Recent statements by the Communications Research Advisory Board address specifically the imminent danger of losing technological viability in the Canadian telecommunications industry.

[17] Mr. D.S. Doyle, president of Digital Equipment of Canada Ltd., has rather strongly proposed that, because Canada is a resource exporter, it is only sensible to develop for export computing technology oriented to the resource industry.

Corporation, General Electric, and Boeing Computer Services use American-located computers to service Canada, some Canadian-based services also operate internationally with much success. In particular, companies such as Systems Dimensions Ltd. (SDL) and I.P. Sharp Associates do a large segment of their business in the foreign markets, accessing computers situated in Ottawa and Toronto. It was recently announced that SDL will install its first U.S. computer in Washington, D.C. in order to meet growing sales in the large East Coast market.

It would appear crucial that Canadian data servicers continue to expand their expertise in more applications geared to network services. With the new developments in packet switching and satellites leading to the interconnection of the various networks, a new international market-place is indeed created. However, without a more adventurous attitude in software development, the loyalty to Canadian data services may be set aside as users increasingly switch to superior American software products. Because the sheer number of U.S. computer professionals (853,000 American workers versus approximately 95,000 Canadians performing similar jobs) renders across-the-board competition from Canada impossible, it is essential that new areas in computer communications be developed for marketing not just in Canada but internationally.[18]

With the increased use of computers and the rising requirement for problem-solving software, it has often been forecast that the 1980s will be the age of software. In line with this, many see the suppliers of hardware falling behind in offering economical software to suit particular applications. To fill this market, suppliers of turnkey systems will emerge, combining hardware and software to meet a user's needs in a unified package. While this is a likely scenario, there are developments on the horizon which will surely affect the long-term trend in the way instructions will be stored in computers. Our present reliance on software to instruct computers what to do will probably give way to solid state applications modules where programs will be coded directly on semiconductor chips. This trend is evident already, as manufacturers view the use of microcoded instructions and "firmware" chip technology as a means of not only enhancing system performance but also concealing the operating system commands from competitors.

There are also many U.S. software packages that have required many years of development at great cost and which are readily available through networks. It would seem to be a waste of time to build similar services in Canada for the sake of "self-sufficiency." For instance, the lead times for development of large-scale bibliographic data bases by U.S. firms, for example, Lockheed and Systems Development Corporation, are such to preclude the duplication of

---

[18] The American estimate appears in an American Federation of Information Processing report, *Information Processing in the U.S.*, October 1977, while the Canadian estimate appears in the C/CS reference cited in footnote 13.

similar systems in Canada, if we are wise.[19] Also, operating systems software is usually manufacturer-supplied and included in the sale or lease of a computer. Because of this, specialized applications software may provide a greater opportunity. While the service bureau segment of the Canadian computing industry is healthy, a positive outlook would indicate even further expansion given the appropriate planning. The success of the data service industry has been accomplished without a great deal of government regulatory intervention. It remains to be seen whether it will continue on its own or require incentives against the use of foreign computing. The extent to which further regulation may be needed cannot be identified at this time.

Technology and management style

If, in the case of multinational corporations, Canadian installations were rapidly shut down in favour of American head office computing, many factors would enter into a policy to deal with the situation. Further tariffs, taxes, or tolls placed on data crossing the border might inhibit some migration, but the problem may be much deeper. In many cases, it is questionable that managers are centralizing their accounting, audit, and data processing functions only because the technology has recently begun to make it cheap and easy to do so. The actual cause may have more to do with a particular management style which simply works best with all the main actors forming a local, close-knit team. This could be as much an explanation of the transborder business as the low cost of generating tapes in Canada and flying them to parent computer centres in the United States. It could be that companies whose management operates in a highly centralized mode will pay to maintain that style, and that adding financial penalties for this may not deter the committed from moving the data out of Canada as usual.

An info-pact

Many who are working toward solving problems of transnational data regulation have called for the initiation of bilateral agreements as a means of reducing the number of discrepancies on a nation-to-nation basis. Because of their trade record and geographical proximity, Canada and the United States would seem to be likely candidates. One could see the negotiations for something vaguely resembling the auto-pact dragging on for years amidst the international turmoil. It might be that multinational interest groups would lobby against the setting up of bilateral agreements, since it is in the best corporate interest to standardize as much as possible the systems and procedures of multinational management information systems. The technology enables this, but a series of

---

[19] Marketing and customer support of the American-based bibliographic services are available in Canada (e.g., Infomart) as are Canadian-developed services such as those offered by QL Systems Ltd.

bilateral agreements, all likely to differ somewhat, could be a mitigating force. However, at a company-by-company level, agreements have been made which do account for the apparent need to foster domestic computer communications growth. For example, the rate structure approved by the CRTC, which applies to the interconnection of Datapac with Telenet and Tymnet, favours the use of Canadian computers by Canadian users. It is simply made more expensive to go across the border for some processing applications.

Reaction to data barriers

It has been suggested that U.S. retaliation could occur if Canada were to erect harsh data barriers which would virtually prohibit American interests from processing Canadian data in the United States. One wonders what form such retaliation might take if limited to the computing industry. Of course, such services as data base access, credit information storage, and electronic funds transfer might be denied. U.S. government or industry could always shut off the supply of hardware, but all of this is really very doubtful. It is clear that the United States has much to offer others through its computing industry, and this must surely be recognized by policy makers here as well as in other nations. The advantages in health, education, research, and many other areas that can be acquired through computer communications have been stated elsewhere many times. For these advantages to come about, it is of great importance that the flow of data across borders not suffer from political obstruction. This is not to say that certain policies may not be required in some areas to foster national economic development. With the realization that computer communications control economic resources, it is important that these resources not come under regulation through political action which focuses only on the technology. If a problem seemingly exists regarding the flow of certain data over national boundaries, then it is important to first distinguish between the data involved in the problem and the computer network providing for its transmission. While it may be simpler to control the technology, the actual source of conflict may go unattended. So far, Canadian jurisdictional concern over data flows has not created a great deal of disturbance, even though in international circles, Canada is sometimes incorrectly singled out as a leader in imposing constraints on the free flow of transborder data. As time passes, Canada may even acquire a "softer" stance more in keeping with its international image of openness.

Data haven Canada

While many more countries continue to press for data protection legislation, Canada might adopt the stance that information is the property right of people rather than government, and that it is the responsibility of government to protect this right. Transnational information exchange must be viewed in terms of the long-range benefits which will accrue for all peoples. This is a strongly contrasting position with the many nations which have taken action to keep data only within their borders for short-term economic gain. Believing that data walls will aggravate trade and co-operation among nations, Canada could extend an open-border policy so far as to encourage the recognition of Canada as a "data haven."[20]

Canada's potential in this area has been recognized in the 1970s by a number of U.S. organizations making public their preferences for storing sensitive data in "peaceful" Canada. For instance, the American Council of Education recognized that data it considered confidential could be stored in Canadian computers and thereby avoid subpoena in legal cases. Similarly, evidence related to the illicit use of drugs in the United States was stored on tape in Canada to evade subpoena by the courts.[21] While these cases may be extremes, the underlying rationale is not unlike that of the Swiss who for some time have operated what might be called a money haven. In establishing the money haven, the Swiss created legislation which bars the storage outside Switzerland of information on Swiss business and banking practices. Recognizing also the parallel with island tax havens, others mention the possible creation of off-shore, pirate computer-data havens as a way to avoid restrictions on data storage and transmission.

It is noteworthy that the American Federation of Information Processing Societies Panel on Transborder Data Flow observed that there is a real possibility that countries with minimal data protection laws will become data havens.[22] However, the means of verifying whether domestic organizations are indeed complying with written law is not well advanced. Because of this, organizations will probably be able to evade local requirements and really not need to resort to data havens.

International arbitration

International conflicts will most surely increase as more and more nations undertake to build barriers to the free flow of computer data. Because the problems are so complex, it has been suggested that an organization such as the International Telecommunications Union, an arm of the United Natons, institute a series of meetings to iron out the problems and draw up laws on jurisdictional rights to information. Such a Conference on the Law of Communications would be loosely modelled on the U.N. Law of the Sea talks held the past several

---

[20] The data haven concept surfaces regularly in discussions about transnational data flows. For a brief introduction, based on the views expressed by George Fierheller at the OECD symposium in Vienna, see "Is Canada a Data Haven?" *Computerdata,* December 1977, pp. 58-59.
[21] Ithiel de Sola Pool, "International Aspects of Computer Communications," *Telecommunications Policy,* December 1976, pp. 33-49.
[22] Panel on Transborder Data Flow, *Observations on Transborder Data Flow,* American Federation of Information Processing Societies, May 1978.

years.[23] One might well question the utility of such an approach, however, given the slowness of the sea talks in coming to solutions. One could see such a conference shape up, though, with members of the developing nations joining forces to fight "informational elitism." It is the developed world which has built the technological infrastructure of sufficient strength to become self-reliant in computer communications in the 1980s. With the exception of countries such as Saudi Arabia, soon to be the first nation with all-computerized telephony, most of the Middle Eastern, Asian, and African countries are at the mercy of the developed nations to transfer computer communications technology. In a global society which increasingly relies on high technology computer communications as a factor in economic survival, Canada, too, may be on its way to greater economic domination by the United States and other more technologically and economically aggressive nations.

The issues we have discussed are important, but the data so far collected by the various interested parties do not provide a very complete picture of computing patterns between Canada and the United States. The surveys on which much current analysis is based draw from such a small sample that it is impossible to infer long-term trends from them. The surveys and calculations of the C/CS, while indicative of trends, do not give near-conclusive evidence that a problem does exist in Canada's future. While it has been shown that migrations of Canadian computing power out of Canada to the United States have occurred, the magnitude of impact is not known. That is to say, if it is shown that a company has added the use of a foreign computer to its operations, it is critical that the nature of the application be known. It is one thing to do a monthly literature search and quite another to run all pay-roll, accounts, and marketing applications of a large manufacturer on a foreign computer. The growing use of mini and microcomputers will also add to the difficulties of assessing the scope of computing as major population counts, such as the CIPS survey, exclude computers of less than one-thousand-dollar-a-month average rental value. Nevertheless, the task must be done.

Assumptions about future shifts in computing from Canada to the United States are difficult to establish based on the available time series. For instance, the data in support of the C/CS forecasts exhibit cyclical fluctuations through the early 1970s, which make an extrapolative curve fit difficult. Dispensing with the time series and armed with an appreciation of the possible range of alternatives, an institution should undertake a survey of the major corporate computing environment in Canada. This research would provide badly needed data for policy analysis. Such an approach would, of course, entail the open co-operation of the companies involved.

---

[23] This has been discussed in, among other places, the U.S. Congress during sessions on the implications of international communications and information. It has also been actively proposed by communications lawyer, John Eger, in his popular paper, *The Brussels Mandate: An Alliance for the Future of World Communications and Information Policy,* February 9, 1978.

As an initial step toward attaining a better understanding of the issues, this first Canadian conference on Canadian/U.S. transborder regulation is being held. The conference must have a practical orientation which would, along with the exploration of basic issues, establish a preliminary agenda for research.

A study to provide the decision makers with a broader basis for action would probably be most successful if conducted by an independent research organization. The investigation would likely benefit from a collaborative effort involving professional societies and interest groups like CIPS and CADAPSO. Also, strong contact with the computing industry would have to be maintained through private researchers such as R.W. Evans Research Corporation, compilers of *EDP In-Depth Reports*.[24] The objective would be to put together the appropriate mix of research skills for a definitive analysis of the issues.

With the rapid changes now occurring, both technologically and politically, it is important that the facts be known for the well-being of the Canadian computing industry and the Canadian population, which in increasing numbers will be affected by the dynamics of this industry in the years ahead.

---

[24] A number of U.S. research companies, such as International Data Corporation and Frost and Sullivan, also examine various market-related aspects of the Canadian computing industry. See, for instance, *Remote Computer Services in Canada* (Frost and Sullivan, October 1976).

Chapter Two

Panel Discussion and Response to the Issues

PANEL DISCUSSION

Morris Crawford, U.S. State Department

I might say that there are many in Washington who do not really believe that there is an issue of transborder data flows. There are many who assert that the real problem is with those who are asserting that there is a problem, like John Eger, Brendan McShane, Oswald Ganley, and myself. I believe that there *is* a problem of transborder data flows. I would like to read to you the concluding sentences of the paper that I have submitted to the workshop, because it sums up what I believe is an important matter that this group today should face up to.

> It is essential that international accommodations be sought that will provide reasonable satisfaction for national information interests. Such accommodations must not inhibit the application and development of computer communications technology. Computer communications technology should be viewed as today's most dynamic and effective factor of production, and be fully recognized for its contributions to improvements in the welfare and well-being of all nations.
>
> While general international arrangements should be pressed, it is particularly essential that Canada and the United States establish acceptable means of assuring one another that information-flow problems arising in the computer communications industries can be resolved to the mutual satisfaction of both countries.

The point that I would like to cover in my brief comments this morning is how do we do it? How do countries like the United States and Canada arrive at satisfactory arrangements whereby the social and economic disturbances that are possible when a new technology is being exploited can be confronted?

First of all, it can be done through international action such as is taking place, or attempting to take place, in the OECD. In the Expert Group on Transborder Data Barriers and the Protection of Privacy that Bill Cundiff has referred to, we are today engaged in drawing up voluntary guide-lines for dealing with the various, and sometimes contradictory, national legislations on personal data protection. The voluntary guide-lines would permit the private companies, whether multinational companies or companies offering data processing services, to continue offering and using the kinds of computer communications services that are cost effective and that provide new job opportunities for individuals in all of the countries that have the services available to them.

Voluntary and non-binding guide-lines are essential, today in particular, because of the uncertainty that all of us face in knowing what kinds of social and economic problems are going to arise as this technology is exploited in the very dynamic situation that is now being developed. There have been many studies in the United States over the past ten years on computer communications, on the implications of the computerization of society. There have been studies on privacy; on electronic funds transfers; on electronic mail; and on the copyright questions. There are a half dozen or so other studies that have been made during the last five years. All of them have one thing in common—they all end up in frustration. We have not been able, despite the application of the best and brightest brains in the United States, to arrive at uniformly accepted conclusions regarding the social and economic consequences of the computerization of society. Even less are we able today to define the international implications in precise terms, in terms that would permit us sensibly and conscientiously to proceed with the definition of the ways in which international law ought to be drawn up to deal with the economic implications of the computerization of society. Not that we do not recognize, not that we do not acknowledge, not that we are not fully aware of the tremendous implications that the computerization of society will have, but we simply do not know how this is going to be worked out in specific terms. It is too soon to write in concrete, to write on stone tablets the way in which societies of the world will operate in the coming 50 years, or in the coming 100 years when the computer will be as important as we know today that it is going to be.

A second way in which we Canadians and Americans can work on the consequences, the implications of the computerization of our societies, is by talking together. This is why I am so pleased to come to this meeting today. It is a beginning, an opportunity to establish a dialogue. There are important problems that Canadians feel that Americans are not sensitive to. This is simply a result of the fact that we are two separate nations. Yet we are interdependent nations. I do not think that there is a problem of excessive dependency. There are those, perhaps in this room, who feel that there are times when there is excessive dependency. But there is interdependency. And the way in which problems of interdependency, problems of neighbours, as the United States and Canada are, can be worked out is by talking to one another about them, to find out what is bothering you, to give us an opportunity to respond to those things, and to inform you of those things that bother us. There is a need for greater study and greater awareness in the United States of the transborder problems that are bothering Canada, that may bother Canada, or that you may see on the horizon that may bother you.

George Fierheller, Systems Dimensions Ltd.

There is an old adage in the computer field, which is of course my background, that the greatest fault one can make is to start designing a system before one has the problem well defined. And I really believe that we are very much in danger of doing exactly that in this particular case. I am very concerned that we are not recognizing that this is not a single problem susceptible, therefore, to some global solution, but is rather a series of problems which people have lumped together, and to which they are trying to come up with some grand answer. I do not believe that there is a global solution. In fact, global solutions to local problems cannot only be dangerous but can be quite counter-productive, particularly, as Morris Crawford pointed out, in a very dynamic, new, and growing field.

I am going to suggest that our first step today be to analyse very carefully what the real problems are, and what the motives are behind people such as myself and such as any of the panelists in recommending solutions, and then to try to design the minimum solution that is needed. Here again, I am going to have to betray a personal bias, because in general, and I do not care if you are talking about engineering a bridge, designing a computer program, or running a government, the best thing to do always is to define the problem very precisely, and then come up with the minimum amount of regulation, legislation, whatever it happens to be, to get the job done. To illustrate the kind of thing I am talking about, I am going to skip through three or four of the major issues and show why they are rather diverse issues or diverse problems, and why the solutions to them, in fact, may have to be relatively tailored.

Take a look at the question of privacy. This is one that is always being put forward to any of the international conferences as being the most important reason for regulation of transborder data flows. In this question alone, one has to recognize that this is very largely a moral, a political, or possibly even a legal question. What tends to happen is that people are confusing the current technology with the fact that this is not effectively a technological question. One of the best statements I have seen on this recently is by the European Computer Services Association, in its brief to the Council of Europe. They were trying, as best they could, to draw a line between the responsibilities of the users and processors of data. The processors of data may well be, and in fact should be, responsible for the security of data, but if you try to regulate all the processing of data, you end up with what is essentially an unenforceable situation. A far better approach, which is the one they proposed, would be to regulate the users of data, if you have to have any regulation at all.

But it concerns me when you try to come out with legislation, for the purposes of protecting individual privacy, which effectively is going to regulate international computerized flow of data. You are simply opening the door to legislation of much broader kinds, which could then regulate all sorts of other data flows. This is what I mean when I say keep the technology separate. That could be regulation of what passes through the mail, regulation of what goes over the telecommunications systems, regulation of what goes over radio—we have seen what happens in some of the behind-the-iron-curtain countries in these areas. If you start regulating the transborder flow of information, then you are opening the door to regulating all these other kinds of media.

Dealing with that problem, is there some kind of a solution to what the real problem is that one might be able to come up with? Of course, we are concerned about the protection of privacy of individuals. But we simply do not know, at this point, how many abuses there actually have been around the world. When I was over at the OECD-sponsored conference in Vienna, I gave a talk somewhat along the same line, and simply asked, a bit off the top of my head, which was not a fair survey, for a show of hands on how many people at that rather large conference had had any personal experience with people's rights being violated because information about them was stored in another country. Not a hand went up; what I had emphasized was not what they had read about, or what they thought might happen, or what they had heard had happened somewhere, but what they had personally experienced and run into. It was not a fair test, but it does indicate that the problem of protection of privacy, while real and definitely one that must be addressed, is one of unknown magnitude. To come up with global or all encompassing solutions to what appears to be a relatively ill-defined problem could be very dangerous. I likened it at one time to being very much like making a decision to close all the banks in the country only because there have been a few bank robberies.

There are things that could be done in that area, such as establishing data ombudsmen or other private organizations in the country with the mandate to monitor what is happening and to correct abuses, when possible, rather than simply coming up initially with legislation that will prevent the use of transborder data flows. Possibly, as I suggested in Vienna, there might also be room for international treaties, allowing for data extradition when personal data are stored in another country. I am not going to belabour that, as I am sure we will get back to all those topics, but in the area of protection of privacy, there are individual things that could be done and logical steps that could be taken that do not involve any global legislation preventing transborder data flow or seriously interfering with it.

A second area sure to be touched on is that of national security. Again, I really suspect that there are very few data involved in this. If countries have to come up with specific or rifle-shot solutions for security, and I do not intend that as a pun, but if they have to come up with particular solutions for that particular problem, that is one thing. But again, trying to come up with a generalized solution simply because there are some areas of sensitive data could be very counter-productive.

A third area is the protection of an industry such as our own, the computer services industry. I was impolite enough to suggest in Vienna that a lot of the reasons being given for wanting to have transborder data protection, and so on, were not, in fact, the reasons usually given or usually put forward as being privacy protection, and so on. They were, in fact, crassly economic, and they were there to protect national computer industries or computer services industries, or whatever. While I do not pretend to speak for the Canadian Association of Data Processing Service Organizations (CADAPSO) on this, certainly I could point out that CADAPSO, as an organization, has never sought that kind of protection, and only recently put in a brief to the federal government saying that it felt this kind of protectionism would, in the long run, be counter-productive. In fact, I will go farther than that. If a lot of the young, pardon me, maybe not-so-young, entrepreneurs who are still around in the field at this point in time cannot do better in developing an industry that can compete internationally than, for example, some of the old line industries, like the textile industry, then heaven knows who in this country can. The industry is not taking the position that it wants international data flows regulated for reasons of protection, tariff barriers, or anything along that line.

Again, there are solutions to that particular kind of problem. If you want to help such an industry in Canada, do it in a very positive way; do not do it in a negative way. If you want to help, for heaven's sake try to make us more competitive with the United States and reduce the duties on computer equipment used in Canada. Maybe you could do things like providing some tax breaks on the allowances for research and development, or giving incentives to universities to share their research and development by sharing in some of the profits that might arise with the industry. You can have the government use more of the industry. There is a long list of these things, and there are positive approaches to particular problems. The balance-of-payments problem is one that was raised, and I am sure that Peter Robinson is going to talk about the potential problems of loss of jobs, outflow of capital, balance of payments, and so on. He has done a very interesting study to which we should pay attention. As Bill Cundiff referenced in his talk, there is a good possibility in this country that we could develop a very fine export industry built not around computer hardware, or any other kind of hardware for that matter, but rather around expertise. Ian Sharp has an organization that has been successful in exporting not only talent but computer cycles from Canada to the United States and elsewhere. Our own firm has done much the same, with about 20 per cent of our business now in the United States, primarily sold from Canada to the United States. Anything that looks as though you are going to throw up barriers certainly is not going to help our industry in the long run. One other thing that is important to bear in mind is that we have always viewed our industry, the computer services industry, as being very much one whose prime mission is to try to help other companies be more productive.

If you do anything that is going to stop Canadian companies from being as productive as they possibly can be, then in all likelihood you are going to worsen the balance-of-payments problem. You may help our industry a little bit, but you will worsen the whole situation quite markedly in the years ahead. That is not the approach I would recommend. There are things you might be able to do that are almost more the open-mouth policy of trying to encourage multinational corporations to be better corporate citizens by processing more in Canada, and so on, but getting into regulation for that purpose certainly concerns me.

In my opinion, the "default option" should always be towards the free international flow of data, and very careful study is needed to ensure that whatever regulations we may have to come up with in certain specific areas are, in fact, better than no regulation at all.

Peter Robinson, Department of Communications, Canada

I have tried to summarize in my position statement some of the concerns that have been expressed by government or pseudo-government bodies, if you like, in regard to the policy questions, Canadian jurisdiction over corporations storing data abroad, and the concern, expressed by the Privacy Task Force, not so much with privacy but with the loss of jobs and balance of payments. Included are several legal questions, such as document authentication, disclosure laws in the various countries, and so on. As to the investigations that we carried out trying to assess the dimensions of the exodus from Canada of computing activity, I have indicated that this year we estimated somewhere in the region of $300-350 million of information processing services being imported, with the possibility of going to $1.5 billion by 1985. I have also indicated the numbers in relation to jobs, about seven and a half thousand, now created outside of Canadian borders to deal with Canadian information processing; these should rise to somewhere in the region of twenty-three thousand by 1985.

I would like to comment on and bring together some of the points that have been made by others on the panel in their formal notes. Mr. Crawford, for example, stated that the information revolution is taking place largely unnoticed. In Canada, certainly there is little public awareness and no public debate on the fundamental changes that are now taking place. Most media, for example, concentrate on the sort of "gee-whiz" type of developments that are taking place. Until this apathy changes, it will be difficult to develop the focus, called for by Mr. Eger, to consider the broad range of related issues. It is primarily because of this lack of focus that the list of investigations cited by Mr. Crawford ends in frustration.

The papers submitted have also given an indication of a number of other issues; I would like to concentrate on what I believe is one of the most, if not the most, important question as far as Canada is concerned. A number of the papers point out that there are clearly different types of data and information flowing across our border, and that we must recognize this in any approach that might be devised. This is an important improvement on my own earlier and very preliminary thinking when I was trying to distinguish between information on the one hand, and data, or the raw material of information, on the other.

I believe we can all agree that there should be a very free and open flow of information in research, in electronic payments, in air transport control, and so on. My concern has been with the wholesale transfer of data—Canadian raw material processed in a foreign location and returned to Canada as summarized information. Will a terminal tucked into foreign, central computer facilities lead Canada into a terminal economy?

I am not so much concerned with the transfer of data abroad. My concern is with the processing of that data, and the impact that will have on Canada. The problem, as George Fierheller pointed out in his position statement, is not from competition in the computer services industry. Canadian service bureaux are second to none. This is an important point: given equal opportunities and conditions with the foreign competitors, there is no fear of the outcome of that competition. The problem, to quote George Fierheller again, is the flow of work load from branches in one country to head offices in another. It could be extended and accentuated with the use of satellite communications, a topic which is touched on in the statement that Andy McMahon submitted.

The problem does not rest with the impact on jobs in the computing field, but extends to managers, accountants, and others who depend on the computer to assist in their work and in their decision making. In his notes, Jim Grant made the point most clearly when he talked about the data and functions related to planning, design, and control. It is the point being made by Hugh Faulkner, when minister of state for Science and Technology: "The danger that industrial and social development will largely be governed by the decisions of interest groups residing in another country." We are at a stage where, if action is taken now, the emigration of these information processing activities from Canada could be stemmed.

As pointed out in Bill Cundiff's working paper, in many firms the organization of computing functions is in a state of flux. It is borne out by the queries I have received regarding Canadian government policies on the consolidation of Canadian computing activities in foreign headquarters. These queries demonstrate the willingness on the part of these companies to comply with government policies and wishes.

There are many other companies that do not appear to be aware of the cross-border impact of their actions. This lack of awareness on the part of the industry is commented on again by Bill Cundiff: he says it is improving; I do not believe that, except in certain limited areas. It was apparent to me at the meeting I attended in Washington.

I also believe there is a very strong, or rather an important, lack of awareness on the part of the systems designer. I am sure that if I were in his shoes I would do exactly as he is doing: design a good system with all the flexibility and benefits afforded by technology. National borders simply would not enter into it as a factor in the design certification. But national borders do exist, and it is becoming increasingly necessary to recognize their existence in corporate, as well as government, policy planning.

As George Fierheller has pointed out, a systems designer cannot really design a system until a problem is defined, nor as he implied, can we develop a policy until we know what the problem is. This is what we were attempting to do in the Computer/Communications Secretariat survey. As Bill Cundiff points out in his working paper, our investigation, and the others that he summarized, did not give us a complete picture, but the signs are quite evident and the potential for a major problem in this area is undeniable.

I am hopeful that this conference can help shed some more light on this issue and others, and will set in motion a series of events that will lead us to a solution. But in this atmosphere of rapid technological development and fundamental structural changes now taking place in society and in our economy, policy makers largely appear to be unaware of the potential problems. Time is not on our side.

J.C. Grant, Royal Bank of Canada

I have three general observations before I get into a few details on this question. In listening to the comments this morning and in reading some of the material, it would appear that information is treated as one category. It is used by various people to mean different things, but it appears to be only one category; I hope to break it down into several categories, which may make it easier to put one's hands around the problem.

The second comment is really a question. Are we concentrating too much on computer communications? They are, in effect, the tools that are available to us in today's economy. Perhaps we should concentrate more on the application of those tools, to either solve business problems or to increase our productivity or standard of living.

The third general observation, a result of some of the comments Peter Robinson was making, concerns the potential job loss. I believe it truly is an economic issue in Canada, and there has been a fair bit of talk about the potential job loss in the computer communications industry. That is just the tip of the iceberg of the potential economic impact on Canada.

In addressing the question of data flow, I would put it into various categories. There are data flows associated with air transport control or meteorological weather information, and nobody would disagree that they should freely cross borders. I think that subject, and there are probably others within that category, should be addressed and rather quickly put out of the way.

The second category is that of data flows associated with financial transactions carried out by banks on behalf of their customers. The bank that I work for has been transporting this sort of data for 110 years, from the sailing ship through to the steam engine through to the airplane. Sometime ago, we installed our first telegraphic circuit; we later entered into Telenet and BankWire; and most recently we went into SWIFT, about which you see a lot of talk in the magazines. That is simply a new way of solving an old problem, as warranted by the type of economy, demands, and time frames we have today.

As we move down this list, we move into some more contentious and probably a little more difficult issues—data flows associated with personal information concerning the health or credit worthiness of individuals. There are some suggestions as to how that can be handled. Surely, reasonable people can sit down and establish some minimum criteria for protection of information on citizens, regardless of the country.

Next are data flows associated with original thinking, which increases knowledge as power and is really a fundamental economic question in Canada. We can include in that original thinking such things in our industry as software development. In the 1978 Datapro survey of software products available in North America, of 870 products, only 11 had a residence in Canada, or 1.2 per cent were Canadian. I am not sure why; I believe the key issue is the data flows associated with planning, design, and control of enterprises.

The impact on Canada of certain categories of data being transmitted across international boundaries can be significant. We should bear in mind the large percentage of Canadian enterprise under foreign ownership and the high overhead cost of conducting business in Canada.

Each of these categories, and there will probably be many others, must be addressed separately, since the parameters or criteria for addressing them are quite different.

The data flows associated with air transport control are quite different from those associated with the planning, design, and control of business enterprises. And I believe the latter are becoming an increasingly larger component of the whole production process, particularly in the secondary industries. As a result of technology, they are also rapidly becoming independent of the location where they are carried out.

Business enterprises, because of competition, tend to follow the path of least cost, particularly when competing in the international market-place. In Canada, we have high overheads, largely resulting from government economic and social policies which tend to make us less competitive. Therefore, unless the environment for conducting business in this country is changed, business enterprises face a dilemma, which could result in more of the planning, design, and control functions moving out of this country into lower cost areas. The control of the actual process, manufacturing of the widgets if you wish, could very well remain local, but the higher type of job opportunities, the challenges, could be carried out at a remote distance.

An example of this, in the financial industry, is the treasurer's function for subsidiaries operating in the country. Information needed to carry out a large part of this function can be available as easily in New York or Chicago as in Toronto or Montreal.

The entire question of transborder data flows is complex, and any efforts to change trends we observe today could have far-reaching implications. It is mandatory to protect national and individual interests, both economic and social, by retaining business functions in this country. An important variable, in the provision of this protection in the lessening of the impact of transborder data flows, is the cost of functioning in Canada versus other locations. Accordingly, the strategy selected must not place even greater stress on cost relationships.

The first obvious solution to create economic balance is to reduce the cost in this country. Recognizing that the cost of doing business is not fully variable in the short term, we must then proceed to slow down the impact by setting targets, by compromise if necessary. As the last resort, if targets and compromise are not effective, legislation may have to be considered. This would require very careful planning to ensure it does not place even greater upward-cost pressure on doing business in this country.

Brendan McShane, consulting specialist

I would like to touch upon the issue of privacy, as far as some of the national legislation is concerned. It appears as if most of the European countries, when dealing with the privacy issue domestically and internationally, are now establishing what they call "data protection boards" or "data ombudsmen," or as one person said, as far as Germany was concerned, "data *Fuehrer.*"

In our rush to protect people's individual rights, we are overlooking, and creating to a certain extent, another monster with these protection boards. When you look at the legislation, you do not see too much as far as guards against the guardians. A recent report has come out pertaining to Sweden and dealing with its five years of activity in data protection. Luckily, it has a very good man, Jan Freese, who is in charge, but I am a little bit concerned about what happens when there is not a Jan Freese in a position of such power. When you establish a bureaucracy that can look both ways into your personal life, I become very much concerned. If Canada is looking at the privacy problem, I think it should pay particular attention to this area.

As far as this morning is concerned, we ought to broaden our horizons. The long-term issue is not computer communications, that is, simply the hardware. What we are really talking about is information per se, and information is a commodity both domestically and internationally. That means information in all its guises, and it applies to all the media, broadcasting, newscasting, film, television, corporate data, anything that is going across communications vehicles.

If Canada is going to do something, it should broaden the horizons of its study and look at its own information policy. At the moment, Canada is working on the OECD guide-lines. Will these guide-lines only be applicable to automated data? If it goes into broadcasting and newcasting, it should note what is happening in that area as far as UNESCO is concerned. It should look at the broad spectrum and come out with its own information policy, not simply a niche of it.

I have not heard anybody talk today about the Third World. I would like to, and perhaps later on someone else will. If we believe everybody who is talking about the post-industrial society—moving from the manufacturing type of society into the service type of economy—the key build up in that area will be the management and transfer of information. In France, recently, we have seen somewhat restrictive legislation. We have also seen the development of an inter-European network for information, a sort of EEC on information. Zeroing in on the Third World, information is key to its development. Canada is a major trader with the Third World in all aspects and could be an even greater trader as far as information is concerned. When you look at your policies on information, look at your market-places as they are going to be in the future, not as they are now, and at what you will be developing in the future with the lesser developed nations.

Bill Cundiff made a good point this morning when he talked about software as a special niche. It is probably the most important niche in this whole area. I talk of software in the larger context, not only software in computers but software in broadcasting, programming, and so on. Here is where the individual is more important than probably even the corporation and the money behind that corporation. It is the individual entrepreneurship and the individual idea in the manipulation of the information that is important. Therefore, you should develop more, and perhaps the Institute for Research on Public Policy should develop more, of the idea as far as that special niche is concerned in information.

The last part I would like to talk about is the idea of a data pact. It is worth pursuing, quite frankly. The approach is a good one, even if you do not completely fulfil what you want. I am concerned with what is happening in this area. To give you an idea, let me read you something. It comes from Brazil and talks about the country's policy on informatique and what recently happened. In Brazil, if you do not know, they have a board called CAPRE that looks at all applications in and out of the country, as far as information processing technology is concerned. On May 2, they issued a new procedure for all persons who want to do electronic data processing with Brazil. They say you have to "file an application with CAPRE, and that the establishment of international systems for data processing will be subject to previous approval by CAPRE, which will decide if the proposed system is compatible with the objectives and national information policy. The approval of such systems shall only be granted if it is for specific aims and for fixed periods of up to three years, and renewable every three years thereafter. The approval mentioned previously shall be requested through proper papers, schedules which can be picked up free of charge from CAPRE, which will analyse the application, having in mind mainly the protection of the Brazilian labour market, the interest of government organs, Brazilian companies, and the desirability of free exchange of information respecting individual rights of privacy. Users of existing systems shall have to file with CAPRE petitions for approval of their systems within ninety days, counting from the date of publication of this resolution by means of proper papers and schedules indicated."

This is the way one nation is beginning to deal with what it considers to be the issues. I would like to see the United States and Canada try a different approach, a more talking approach, as Morris Crawford was saying today. I have been to many of these conventions, including Brussels and all the others, and this is the first one that I have seen where some of the major issues have started to come out on the table. I think it is good, because if Canada and the United States cannot settle their perceived or actual problems, then what is going to happen to the rest of the world?

Andrew McMahon, Bell Canada

There are probably a few things that the panel is in agreement on. There seems to be an increasing discussion on the growing question of bureaucracy, and if there is any area that is Canada's expertise, this is surely it. So we have some knowledge to export in this country, and we would be pleased if any of our visitors from foreign countries would like to have it.

Somebody mentioned Saudi Arabia this morning. We had a recent situation where we negotiated a contract for the design and management of the telephone system in Saudi Arabia. We beat a consortium of international companies for a contract worth about $1.1 billion, and I am probably not exaggerating to say that it was less difficult to negotiate that contract with the Saudis than it was to get through to the various bodies in Canada, including the Combines Investigation Branch, the Human Rights Commission, and the Canadian Radio-television and Telecommunications Commission.

You wonder sometimes whether or not we have other areas, other than bureaucracy, in which we have developed skills. I hope that out of this conference today comes some leaning toward the recognition of the rightful role of government in establishing policies and workable guide-lines, freeing up the entrepreneurs to do what can and should be done. Those boundaries seem to have been severely clouded in the last period of time where there is a constant pressure to try to second guess the entrepreneurial environment within the country.

Let me just make a few comments with respect to the issue at hand. We should proceed on the assumption that technology is here and is making it easier and cheaper to communicate internationally. For all practical purposes, there really is no telecommunications barrier existing today, from a technological point of view, between Canada and the United States or any other country.

In this continent of North America, specifically in Canada and the United States, we have lived rather easily for many years with the issue of transborder flow of communications. We have a long history of co-operation between Canada and the United States in transborder voice traffic; we share a common switching hierarchy throughout the entire North American continent; we have a numbering system that is mutually interdependent; we have mutually interdependent network management and control; and we have complete interchange of all necessary control information for emergency situations. There has, in effect, been a total integration of the American and Canadian networks. If you operate the phone on a long distance call, whether it is to Pierrefonds, Vancouver, or California, the pull of the dial or the touch of the pad operates the equipment in any part of the North American continent, regardless of the location or of who built the equipment. It is a free and complete interchange of traffic, and there is one set of standards throughout the entire network.

There are, however, different aspects with respect to how the environment operates, particularly from the point of view of rating. There are different geography and population patterns and regulatory outlooks between Canada and the United States, and this has led to different rating structures between the two countries. For example, in Canada basic telephone service rates generally tend to be lower than they are in the United States, and long-haul transmission or long distance rates are generally higher here than in the United States.

The difference is partly due to geography and partly due to costs, but it is mainly due to a different emphasis in using long distance revenues to support the higher cost of providing local service.

Another issue that is a fact of social and regulatory life in Canada is that there has been an intense emphasis in this country on the concept of price averaging. The purpose has been to ensure that there is equal access to all communications services for all Canadians, wherever they happen to be. The result is that rates in densely populated areas exceed the cost of providing those services, and the reverse is true in the more remote locations where you do not generate enough revenues to cover the cost. I do not argue with this at all as being a desirable and a beneficial social objective. But it is one we have to recognize exists in this country of ours.

The cross-border voice network has been developed in such a way as to permit a free flow, recognize the desire for North-South as well as East-West communications, and in effect, set up the networks so that they act as one, the only difference being in the rating philosophies that exist between the two countries. I think this is consistent with government objectives as they are set out in Bill C-24, *An Act Respecting Telecommunications in Canada* (introduced in the House of Commons, January 24, 1978).

In dealing with the issue of data rates, you move more toward a private-line type of environment or a dedicated facility environment than you do in the normal voice networks, and there are a lot of ways in which you can set up rating structures between two countries. If you look at it from a narrow, nationalistic point of view, when you communicate between two countries, you want to maximize the length of the facility that is provided in your country.

The agreement that has been negotiated between ourselves and the United States and has been in existence for years says that you establish the shortest distance between the two points to be connected, and you cross the border at that point and divide the revenues accordingly. This takes away the artificial kind of thinking that creates artificially high rates, and we can create artificially high rates enough otherwise without having to try to do that.

I point that out only as an example of the fact that individual private enterprise, left to its own ability, ingenuity, and bottom-line discipline will normally come up with the kind of solution that will be marketable. That has happened in the private line connections between Canada and the United States, with its shortest distance philosophy as opposed to the maximum through your own country.

As mentioned earlier, we have moved more recently on interconnection agreements between Canada and some of the newer, value-added networks in the United States. We want to move, to the maximum extent possible, toward an integrated kind of rating structure as opposed to a philosophy of end-on-end rating structures and duplicate bills from each individual supplier of the service.

In the long run, integrated kinds of rate structures, referred to in the industry as joint through-rates, probably lead to the most cost-effective kind of solution. We are moving fairly successfully toward that direction with some of the value-added networks in the United States.

One of the areas I would like to touch on briefly, and of major concern to Canada, is the field of satellite communications and the very real possibility of excess capacity being available in the United States in the early eighties.

At present, all the Canada-United States traffic is carried by terrestrial facilities. There are a limited number of jointly agreed-to border crossing points between the two countries. However, the introduction of a large number of satellite systems in the United States, coupled with the possible wide-spread utilization of privately owned earth stations in Canada, could lead to very severe fragmentation and cream skimming of the Canadian market-place.

A possible result could be that intra-Canadian traffic could be routed via private earth stations and American satellites. American-based multinational firms, for example, could route all their traffic to the United States via those satellites, including Canada-to-Canada traffic, thereby by-passing Canadian networks completely. This is tied in with the concern that, with clear indication of excess satellite capacity in the United States in the eighties, there will be dumping of that excess capacity across the Canadian border.

Because of their huge volumes of traffic, American satellites can potentially off-load to Canada at greatly discounted rates. And if these satellites are permitted to transmit directly to Canada and land signals from American satellites onto Canadian earth stations, it will probably mean the death of a domestic satellite industry. And even more important in the long run, it makes Canada totally dependent on a foreign country, albeit a very friendly foreign country, for a significant sector of this telecommunications technology.

There is an application from the RCA Corporation now before a regulatory body here in Canada for such licensing of ground stations for CATV purposes. Therefore, the concerns are real.

There are a couple of policy objectives that we would see to be essential, and when I say policy objectives, there is a difference between policy objectives and massive bureaucracy or regulation. If there is a clear understanding on the part of both countries, or whatever countries are involved, as to what the national objectives and basic guide-lines are, then it should be left to the individual companies and participants in the scheme to satisfy the various governments and regulatory authorities that they, in fact, accept the obligation and are living within the intent of the objectives. There are three, really: (1) traffic originating and terminating within a country should be carried on facilities that are provided by that country. And that is true, whether it is Canada-to-Canada traffic or United States-to-United States traffic; (2) the signals from American satellites should not be licensed to land in Canada and vice-versa, except under reciprocal agreements, such as defence and security, and then at ground stations that are owned by regulated telecommunications common carriers; and (3) international non-proprietary standards or protocols are essential to remove the barriers to effective transborder data flows.

We, in Canada, have played a role over the last couple of years in attempting to get international standards in the growing area of packet switching, and we have been reasonably successful in so doing. Certainly that is not the end of the road. We have to adopt the philosophy that as many of the technological barriers as possible should be cleared to enable effective communication to take place so that there is no technological limitation. In my mind, common standards throughout the world, non-proprietary standards, are absolutely essential in order to achieve that. And that includes standards that are agreed to by the major equipment manufacturers as well as the telecommunications providers.

We are facing a very strong clash here in the next few years, where as you merge together the technologies of computers and communications, you merge together a philosophy from the computer industry, that essentially works with proprietary standards in order to enhance each participant's position in the market-place, as opposed to the telecommunications industry, that essentially works with non-proprietary, published international standards. And that confrontation is now beginning to come to a head. I hope that it will be the faction that favours common, non-proprietary, international standards that will win. It is essential if we are to ensure that the technological barriers not be there.

The close co-operation that has existed between Canada and the United States has helped us provide and maintain a first-class voice telecommunications system in North America, and if we extend those kinds of philosophies, we can probably do the same in data and record communications.

It is reasonable to point out that the completely free flow of information that has existed, and has come to be taken for granted between Canada and the United States up to this point, has developed and grown under a philosophy of absolute minimum government intervention and minimum regulation. There is every indication it may change, and I am not exactly sure as to how it will change for the better.

As one of the world's significant trading nations, we should realize that the increased flow of data opens up a significant number of opportunities for us. The concept of a data haven has been mentioned; I am not sure that we have the intestinal fortitude in this country to embark upon that kind of a pact, but it is a significant business opportunity that is certainly worth exploring. It could not be explored without positive indication and support from the federal government.

John M. Eger, attorney-at-law

If you have done your homework, you know that the Brussels Mandate is not the name of a new rock group nor is it simply the title of a speech given in the city by the same name. What, perhaps, you do not know is that the Brussels Mandate is not a new bureaucracy. We all seem to agree that we have more than our share of that. It is not an intellectual think tank, it is not a trade association; if it is anything, it is the administrative sponsor of at least one conference which was held in June of this year in London, and it is a symbol or reference point of the true need for an alliance of world communications; alliance among all peoples across all borders. I want to return to that briefly, and hopefully during the course of the day, share with you my sincere belief of why an alliance may be necessary. As Peter Robinson points out, the clock is running against us, and that is all of us: manufacturers, suppliers, consumers large and small, indeed governments.

Let me make four points. I concur with the others that the problem is that the computer, in a sense like the cotton gin of an earlier era, is transforming the developed societies of the world. It seems that the present trend of world development, from an agrarian to an industrialized to a post-industrialized information-based society, is the route toward which most nations seem to be heading.

As you know already from some of our studies, in the United States we have estimated that somewhere between 20 and 46 per cent of our gross national product is directly a result of the production, use, storage, and dissemination of information. Information indeed has value; it is a commodity that we are beginning to recognize can be bought and sold, like any other commodity in world trade. Because world economies are inextricably intertwined, we are beginning to recognize that how successfully we develop our information policies, and how successfully we encourage others to develop global information policies, will determine the kind of society and the kind of government we will have.

Those are pretty big stakes. The problem is that nobody really knows what the value of information is, has defined information, or has studied the transnational economics of communications sufficiently. Yet everybody seems to be rushing headlong to find some quick fix, some regulation to put in place, with which to control the flow of information in some amorphous way, so as to control the wealth that information represents for the citizens of any given nation state.

You have to applaud, and I do, the concern of policy makers of governments for the privacy of their citizens and the sovereignty of their nation. But the problem is much broader than that, which brings me to my second point that regulations, once in place, are not easily removed. I served on President Ford's Ad-Hoc Committee for Regulatory Reforms. We began to look at the sheer size, bulk, and cost of regulations, which have grown exponentially since

1887 when the railroad-hating farmers came to Washington, and we created something called the Interstate Commerce Commission. In the last twenty years, we created some two hundred and sixty new agencies, departments, or commissions and eliminated about twenty-one. We now have something like forty-five hundred federal forms which are filled out by business and individuals every year and which fill eleven Washington monuments; according to a paperwork commission recently, only about a quarter of those forms are even read: they go in boxes and get filed in some archives.

The cost is estimated to be in the low end at $60 billion a year and in the high end at $130 billion a year. So much so that General Motors, in evaluating its cost of government, finds that it costs industry $1.6 billion a year in what they call unnecessary government; along with other industries, they have set this matter of regulation, or excessive regulation, on something called the business round-table.

They have, together with sincere government officials—certainly the Ford campaign was run on the promise of deregulation, and the Carter campaign as well—tried to deregulate and strip away the layers of unnecessary regulations. I tell you that even within the continental United States, with the joint effort of government and business, it has not been done and the prognosis is dim.

If we have a patchwork of legislation around the world designed to protect privacy, security, sovereignty, laws dealing with censorship, tariffs, protocols, what have you, and if they are put in place nation-state to nation-state with different goals, with a different understanding of the size and shape of the problem, what a dilemma it will be, in the not too distant future, to try to unravel all of this.

I am going to skip to my fourth point which is simply that, in attempting to arrive at solutions and in discussing this issue as we have thus far this morning, it is important to recognize that it is a world problem. Information is emerging as one of the world's vital resources; let us deal with it that way.

In the process, let us recognize that, yes, we are citizens of Canada, of the United States, of Japan, of Saudi Arabia, of Brazil. We are also citizens of the world, in a sense. As difficult as it is to get out of our racial, sexual, economic, or national security blankets, the fact of the matter is that the economies of the world have been drawn together, and the technology of computers, communications, and transportation has blurred the national borders.

In addressing solutions, it is important to increase the dialogue. This is not a problem to which we are going to find a quick fix; it is a problem that will be with us for the next twenty years, at least; it is a problem that involves all people; it is a problem that has attached to it excessive, burdensome costs to both personal and individual, as well as economic, freedoms. Therefore, if we do nothing else, we need to increase the dialogue; we need to ensure that there is an informed electorate, if you will, in every nation state, that begins communicating, first within its own national government, and then hopefully in international forums at which decisions will be made and agreements hammered out.

And lastly, because of the immensity of the issue, be courageous, be creative, do not try to pigeon-hole ideas nor attach boxes to them, so that they fit the normal patterns. We are breaking new ground and we are crossing new thresholds. I conclude by citing Cyrus Vance, who upon his return from Paris last year where he attended the North-South conference, said: "We have ceased an era in which the decision was whether or not to co-operate; the question now is how to find the means and institutions with which to co-operate."

RESPONSE

Peter Robinson

I should be responding to some of the first remarks of Andy McMahon, but as I find myself at a bit of a loss, I will pass that one. Brendan McShane mentioned the Third World; I have just come back from Torremolinos, Spain, where there is a Conference on Strategies and Policies in Informatique, where there is a large gathering of developing countries, and so on. To a large extent, it was a political forum rather than a forum for getting down to the guts of some of these issues. But to indicate the sort of concerns of some of these developing countries, there was a draft resolution being passed around which drew attention to the concerns of the developed countries for the privacy of individuals, and drew a parallel between that and, if you like, the data protection of the developing states. One of the clauses of this draft resolution was to the effect that the conference should proclaim the unalienable right of all countries to have access to all information stored in their country by any other country.

That resolution in those terms will not be passed, but it does indicate the very growing concern, on the part of developing countries, over the information explosion that is now taking place. As John Eger said, it is a world problem, not only a Canada/United States problem, nor indeed only a developing countries/OECD-membership type problem.

William Loewen, Comcheq Services Limited

Mr. Crawford, if a situation existed in the United States where as much as 90 or 95 per cent of your oil industry and 60 or 70 per cent of your manufacturing industry were foreign controlled, would you not say that your country should perhaps reconsider your suggestion of voluntary guide-lines and take a hard line that was much more nationalistic? That is my feeling, and I would like to know if you would understand and agree if Canada took that stand?

Morris Crawford

I am not sure of your percentages of dependence in regard to oil, but I would note that the United States is very kindly disposed to Saudi Arabia these days, and I quite agree that interdependency is a factor that one nation must take into consideration in the modern world. The way to approach these questions of interdependency is through collaboration, discussion, and mutual accommodation. The maximum degree of voluntarism should be sought with the minimum degree of government intervention. I have been a bureaucrat all my life, except for a few years when I was a school teacher, and I see the attitudes and the problems of bureaucracy from the bureaucrat's side. I believe that maximum non-intervention on the part of bureaucrats is desirable and essential for the continuation of freedom and the common welfare of the people of the United States. I would suggest this is also true for the people of Canada, and I would extend that to the mutual problems that exist between Canada and the United States.

Gaston Beauséjour, ministère des Communications, Québec

Mr. Crawford has mentioned that transborder data flows are seen, or are starting to be seen, as a problem by Canada. Are they seen as a problem by the United States, and if so, how? What kinds of problems are foreseen?

Morris Crawford

The problem of transborder data flows is seen by the United States as a very real one; it is seen in somewhat spotty terms. I commented earlier that there were some people in the United States who did not recognize them as a problem at all. I do not think this is true, and there are several Americans here today who are among those attempting to bring the problem to the attention of the top leaders in the United States government. I commented also on the attitude of the American business community toward transborder data flows, because I have had personal contact with a large number of American business leaders about this very issue, trying to get from them an answer to the question that you have asked me this morning. They are very concerned about the possibility of restrictions on transborder data flows. American multinational companies, like Canadian multinational companies, like European multinational companies, are deeply dependent on computer communications for their corporate planning. Some companies are dependent on their marketing of computer communications. Among the American company leaders I talked to, there is a very real awareness of the problems they would face if there were any restrictions on the flow of international data.

By the same token, there is an uncertainty on their part about what is going on in the world and what to do about it. And the uncertainty varies, depending on the company. Many companies that are dealing in personal data, such as credit card companies, hotels, airlines, financial corporations, banks, are very much aware of the personal data legislation that is being passed in the European nations today, and they are very much concerned about that. Other companies, less dependent upon the flow of personal data, are more ambivalent in their reaction to what is specifically happening in the world today.

To repeat my original point, there is no question about the multinational companies' interest in transborder data flows. Their livelihood depends on it, and their corporate planning cannot exist without it.

Eric Cowan, Privy Council Office, Canada

I would like to address a question to Mr. Grant. I was interested to see, in the very last part of his paper, that he has put in a good word for legislation. He seems to be suggesting that legislation may be the only answer.

I was not quite sure what he was getting at there. He was very careful to talk about different categories of data flows, so my question has two parts. First, to which kind of data flows was he suggesting that legislation pose as an answer? Second, having said that legislation will require very careful planning, can he tell me how he reconciles these two statements? In particular, could he give me any precedents in the legislation field that would show me clearly what he has in mind for legislation and how legislation could accomplish the objectives he has?

J.C. Grant

I am not sure how to start answering that question. In my comments, I talked about various categories, and said that there are certain categories that should be reasonably easy to define and resolve between Canada and the United States. The prime issue, starting today but particularly more so in the next five years or, in the medium term, ten years, is the question of planning, design, and control of a Canadian business enterprise.

I quoted one example in the financial industry; there are probably others in the basic production process where today we have machine tools and tomorrow we will probably have computer control, basically in the assembly process. It is not inconceivable to have the planning, design, and control of that whole process located in a less costly area. In other words, daily or weekly, you could transmit to your plant which is located here information necessary to run that plant for that day or week, and do all the machine coding necessary to run your production facilities.

This is the area I have concern with, and this is the area where the greatest problem is. There has been a fair bit of talk about this problem in the computer communications industry. Peter Robinson talked about loss of jobs in the hardware, software sector. It is a larger problem than that. In terms of how one may approach it, I came here today to try to better define the problems rather than to look for solutions. There has been some precedent set on transborder flow of goods in the tangible world. While information is intangible, perhaps there are some lessons to be learned as to how the problem has been addressed in the tangible world, in the flow of machines, and those sorts of things.

There is government persuasion, there are tariffs that could be set up, but I am not sure about the mechanisms; legislation would be the last resort. I did not necessarily put in a good word for legislation; it may have to be an alternative if the problem is as large as I think it could be.

Oswald H. Ganley, Harvard University

This meeting has already made a major contribution to the discussion and dialogue about transborder data flows, and at least to my knowledge, it is the first meeting where we have cast away the screen of privacy that has been hanging over these discussions over the last two years, and where we are frankly facing the facts that what we are really talking about are important economic and cultural questions.

Particularly in the economic area, we have further defined here today some of the major questions that are involved, such as employment, balance of payments, building up of domestic industries, and brain drain, although it has not been mentioned directly.

This is terribly important, because once you define more clearly what the real issues are, they can then be looked at, analysed, discussed, and possibly solved. Frankly, I was always a little bit, if not to say very, uncomfortable when testifying, for instance, before congressional committees. I had to say "well, I have the suspicion, or we have a high index of suspicion, that perhaps behind privacy something else might be lurking." This conference is a tremendous contribution and hopefully other groups, including some international organizations, will pick up the example of what has been done here.

Frank Paine, Honeywell Information Systems

This subject, in my mind, breaks down into two major issues. The first issue is an old one in Canada, and that is the cost of production. I see, indeed, a processing facility as a production facility, and I see its problems as being not greatly different from the problems associated with someone who is making shoes, shirts, or any other product. He has to compete, and he has to compete internationally. In Canada, the vulnerability is particularly focused because of the high level of foreign ownership, and the danger with this cost of production is the loss of even high quality jobs, that is to say, management jobs and decision-making jobs. It ultimately leads to the situation where in Canada it will be possible for a company to do business with practically no physical presence. You could see this particularly with products that had high value and low volume.

The remedy for the cost of production lies somewhat in the hands of government, as one of the speakers has already pointed out. And that is easement of the cost of running a production facility, a data processing production facility, in Canada. Those costs are associated with the cost of equipment itself, which is invariably made outside these borders, and that would mean the tariff costs which are added to the Canadian producer, and which the American producer or source producer does not have.

The other costs are the operating costs associated with capital cost allowances, where there can be an improvement, and the tendency or propensity, perhaps, for provinces to add the tax load to the software products of such production. There is an obvious movement in this direction among several of the provinces in this country.

Those costs, plus the labour costs, which are intensified by an increasing tendency for governments to raise their cost of production and cost of employment, are reaching a point where they may be even greater than they are in any of our competing territories.

The second issue is the enforcement of privacy legislation that the United States may enact. If the United States does enact privacy legislation, a problem, in my view, is how to enforce that on behalf of a foreign state across the border. A man with a terminal in Windsor, Ontario, can access a Detroit data base, notwithstanding the fact that Michigan legislation says that particular kind of data base should not be accessed by foreigners.

Daniel Cooper, McCarthy & McCarthy

Could I address a question to Dr. Robinson, and if the gentleman from the Privy Council Office would like to comment, I would be intrigued to have his thoughts. It seems to me that Dr. Robinson, and Mr. Grant as well, has emphasized that while we do not have the available data base for developing and articulating at this stage a national information policy, the problems would tend to be, in the future, primarily economic ones.

An observation: in Canada, the federal government has taken two recent stabs, in proposed legislation, to somehow restrict the flow of data, and I am a little concerned that there is no policy underlying that. One example is in the proposed *Bank Act* revisions, which would provide that banks, Canadian chartered banks, may not transmit data about their customers for processing across the border. The other one is in the proposed overhaul of the competition legislation, which provides that, in relation to any business carried on in Canada, there must be maintained at that place in Canada a description of how the computer system of that enterprise works, including access codes to permit, presumably, the investigators to get into the system.

These are the two recent, concrete examples of government action in this field. They both seem to be directed to enforcement permitting the regulators to have access to the information that they think the business enterprise or the banks should have. Is this valid federal policy? Has anybody articulated that policy? Are there other means to resolve that particular irritant?

Peter Robinson

Could you explain what irritant you are talking about?

Daniel Cooper

Well, for example, in the case of the chartered banks, a number of them, as we all know, do obtain certain kinds of data processing services outside Canada. In the case of the proposed amendments to the *Competition Act,* there is very little discussion about security, or who would pay the service bureau, for example, on whose data banks a certain company's records are maintained for the processing required. Presumably the federal investigators could walk in and start playing with George Fierheller's computer system.

Peter Robinson

I am going to take the usual bureaucratic "out" and pass the buck. The *Bank Act* is the responsibility of the Department of Finance, competition legislation is the responsibility of the Department of Consumer and Corporate Affairs. I, or indeed the Department of Communications, really have no veto power on what either of these departments does in regard to legislation. As to an underlying government policy concerning these legislations, the answer must be that, at the moment, there is no concerted focus on the issues. As I mentioned earlier, we do not have that focus in Canada, and the United States says it does not have that focus. Both in the United States and, to some extent in Canada, we are struggling to develop a focus of this type, but we have not yet achieved it.

Brendan McShane

As far as the United States is concerned, I hate to disagree with Peter Robinson, but in the last three or four months, we have developed a focus. By January 20 of next year, the president of the United States is supposed to report on what the United States information policy should be. I doubt if he will be able to do it in that short period of time. He will probably ask for a little bit more time because it is a complex area. Another thing that is being done, as far as the United States is concerned, is an inter-agency task force where all the government departments are now co-ordinating what they think information policy should be, and are starting to get a hold on the various aspects of it. There is an inter-agency task force set up by the State Department dealing with the international aspects of this. Part of that is a working party of an advisory committee that has public participation. Business and individuals are working towards what the international information policy should be in the United States. The level of consciousness within the United States has risen dramatically, I would say, within the last six months. As you know, sometimes we are a little bit slow, but we come in, in the stretch. We are working very hard in this area, putting the pieces together and coming up with some sort of overall policy.

John Eger

Just a thought. In all respect, Brendan McShane is one of the brightest thinkers, spokesmen in the United States, and a delightful cynic. I have never heard such optimistic views about the U.S. policy process. I share with Peter Robinson a certain sense of hopelessness and empathy, in short, for the way in which the United States and Canada both are struggling with the issue. It is fair to say that both of our countries rely or believe, at least traditionally, in free enterprise, freedom of spirit, and for that reason have not looked as a body politic to government for solutions to most problems.

As a consequence, we are a little bit behind, we are a little bit caught short in looking at the interrelationship of such issues as transborder data flows. And until such time as governments begin cutting across bureaucratic lines of thought and organization in dealing with this issue, there will be no policies.

George Guedarian, CBS

I would like to address my question to Mr. Robinson. One of your major concerns is job losses in case of inter-border transportation. Have you, by any chance, done a study of job opportunities by 1985 and the availability of qualified personnel at that time?

Peter Robinson

We have produced estimates of what we feel will be the growing number of people involved in the information processing activities, and certainly there is a large increase; but that is a part of the question. One of the major problems that has not been mentioned this morning does not devolve on transborder data flows, but is a growing problem in all countries, is the impact of computerization and automation on the work force in general. The concern we have in regard to lost job opportunities in the concentration of information processing abroad, largely in the United States, is perhaps a symptom of that impact on the labour force in general. If I can quote from memory, the seventy-five hundred jobs that we say are being created outside are somewhere in the region of 6 per cent of the total involved in information processing in Canada, whereas the twenty-three thousand I mentioned for 1985 jump up to about 14 per cent of the jobs in Canada. While the absolute value of job losses is increasing, the relative value is also increasing.

George Guedarian

I was at a conference two weeks ago, at which time IBM made a statement on a study they had made that by 1985, I do not remember the number of new jobs created, there will be four hundred thousand jobs available, but not enough personnel to fill those jobs pertaining to the technology. That scares me. Let us assume we cannot transfer data; let us assume we will process everything here in Canada or any other nation. Are there going to be people available who, at that time, will be qualified to fill the jobs? It is a dangerous situation.

W.H. Loewen

You mentioned, Mr. Grant, that financial transactions have been handled internationally for 110 years, which I am sure is true, but possibly the difference now is that financial transactions dealing with transactions between Canadians, in this case, are being handled internationally or on foreign computers. Possibly that is the whole reason for the conference, concerns, and so on, that transactions between nationals are being handled outside that particular country. Would you see the solution as being simply to say that transactions between nationals must be processed within their country?

J.C. Grant

I was referring to a long established practice that transactions, whether between nationals in Canada or carried out, on behalf of a customer in a bank, between a Canadian and someone in another country, have been carried out by various means over the last hundred-odd years. And the fact that today, if we are initiating a transaction in Canada to make a payment on behalf of a client some place in the world, using a new technology should not change the basic business reason. Sometime ago we may have done it by a letter of credit on behalf of the customer.

W.H. Loewen

Could I just interrupt? I mean transactions such as financial collection systems, where a company in Canada, for example, a branch in Vancouver, is trying to transfer funds to Toronto, and it is done through a U.S. computer. It is those transactions, not the international transactions, that have gone on for a long time.

J.C. Grant

Speaking for the Royal Bank of Canada, we have carried out a policy of handling that type of transaction within Canada. I am not sure of the financial industry in general. There may have been a few exceptions when we were initially starting services some years ago, but the principle under which we operate is that that sort of transaction service between somebody in Vancouver and Toronto can, by and large, be handled within our own Canadian network.

W.H. Loewen

Let me, in fact, rephrase it then. Would you see it as being a satisfactory policy, from your point of view, if all transactions between Canadians were processed within Canada, both for banks and for industry?

J.C. Grant

As you are in an international field, you have to be competitive. I cannot speak for the industry in general; I can only state what the policies of my particular organization are. For a whole host of reasons, one of which is economic, we would plan to move that sort of data within our own network. I really cannot comment on what other organizations would do nor on what criteria they would use, but it would seem to make sense that they would be handled within the Canadian network. We have to keep in mind that we are in a competitive world.

J.M. Vaughn, PPG Industries, Inc.

The question raised by the gentleman who asked the question is what denotes a U.S. computer? For example, in the same situation that was earlier posed, if a service bureau which is headquartered in Toronto is now constructing another branch in the United States, and a transaction were to be routed to this service bureau, it very likely could end up being processed on a computer in the United States, should the bureau use the branch to off load at peak periods. Would that constitute an American computer or a Canadian one?

This leads to another decision that needs to be made: whether the problem is really one of moving the data out of the country, that is, the loss of control of that data, having the data reside in another computer in another country; or whether it is having the processing done in another country, with the possible loss of revenue to the country of origin of the transaction.

Peter Robinson

As with most of these questions related to computer communications, the question is a lot easier than the answer. There are always ifs, ands, and buts to add to any answer that one gives. As I tried to indicate, my own concern is not so much with the transfer of data or information, but with the actual processing that is done at the other end of the line, and this encompasses dissemination of the summarized information as well as storage, and so on. But it is primarily the economic impact rather than the fact that some data are stored in a U.S. computer. It is the job loss, the loss of control, again rather than just the mere storage in another country.

J.M. Vaughn

I would like to comment on that last question, regarding PPG Industries, Inc. in the United States and the storage of information down there.

The example you cite, where Canada might take a very narrow view and prohibit such computer use in the United States, would be designed to protect Canadian industry one way or another. However, the alternative to that might be for the customer to buy his own computer, a minicomputer or whatever, and do it in Canada, in which case the device has been purchased from a U.S. industry anyway, and there is in fact no job creation or revenues created within Canada. I think you have to be very careful, when those kinds of artificial barriers are set up, that you have not created great inequalities, or attempted to stamp out a problem that is mythical, in fact. And you could, no doubt, expect that there would be a likewise reaction to such a narrow view to protect American service bureaux and prohibit the opportunity for Canadian bureaux to seek American business.

Brendan McShane

Mr. Robinson, if I could question you on your job loss theory, is this a computer model that you are using, or are these actual facts as far as the job loss is concerned? Are we dealing with a problem or a potential problem? Exactly what are we dealing with? And for the man from PPG, we have a question of trade-offs here. As my friend from Bell Canada said, sure, you can buy the hardware from the United States, bring it back, and process the data, but your main job is to be more productive. The computer services industry in Canada is a pretty ferocious competitor, and its job is to make your industries more productive. It is not an easy question, because you have so many trade-offs that are going on as far as that is concerned.

Peter Robinson

As your question implies, I have as much scepticism as you have in regard to computer modelling. We have not used a computer model to derive our estimates. Perhaps that is a rather poor admission on the part of people who are engaged in this business, but we have not touched the computer. The methodology used has been described in detail in a publication of the Computer/Communications Secretariat, setting out all of the somewhat limited data that we have been able to get, setting out all the assumptions that have been made, and indicating in great detail the ways in which we made these estimates.

William Cundiff, Institute for Research on Public Policy

Regarding the methodology that was used by the Computer/Communications Secretariat, it is not a computer model per se, but a lot of the operations in it certainly could be computerized as far as calculating the projections based on certain time series. In those time series, we see some cyclical fluctuations that make it difficult to fit curves to them. We have discussed this before with Al Shackleton and Peter Robinson, and the particular caveats that I issue in my paper are based on those discussions. While it is not computerized, it is a calculating approach and certainly amenable to that sort of analysis.

Gordon B. Thompson, Bell Northern Research

It has been said that if you hunt rabbits and tigers you have to keep your eye out for tigers. However, if you hunt tigers, you do not have to keep your eye out for rabbits. I would suggest that what I have been hearing this morning is a bunch of rabbit hunters in tiger country, but unfortunately, the tigers are yet to be born.

If the whole information technology thing really has its profound socio-economic impacts at the levels that we have been talking about today, we might as well forget about it. It is a rather insignificant sort of adjunct to our present enterprises. We really have to be very careful here to make sure that we do not inhibit the birth of the tiger. The tiger is really what we are looking for. If we are not careful, we could end up building walls to protect the rabbits and kill off the tigers. I am for tigers and let us make sure that we get these tigers growing. If we do not learn how to use this technology to make it so we can really create wealth with it, instead of shovelling around the stuff we have got, we are in real trouble. I leave you that concern. I do not care how many service bureau jobs get moved to the United States; if neither one of us, Americans or Canadians, can figure out how to make it so that John Q. Public can get rich because he is using this stuff, we are in trouble.

Unidentified Speaker

I would like to ask Mr. McMahon a question about his aversion to satellite communications being offered to Canadians by American firms. Is that because he is afraid that the Canadian satellite industry is not ready to compete with the American one, and how is that of benefit to the Canadian consumer?

Andrew McMahon

We are dealing realistically with the question of economies of scale. Satellite technology is such that you cannot do it in increments as you can most evolutionary type technology; you do it in massive chunks. The massive chunks centre around $25 million launch costs and $25 million birds. You are looking at, for example, in Canada's program or in the Satellite Business Systems (SBS) program, which are approximately the same, at roughly $100 million increments of investment. It is a simple matter of economics and economies of scale. If you have a limited market, as in Canada (about 8 per cent of the United States market), you will not be able to generate sufficient size or revenues to be able to support the investment of the hundred million dollars which has to be replaced, incidentally, every seven years. So you are at a basic decision point. Either you decide to withdraw entirely from that sector of telecommunications or you decide to get in. If you decide to get in, the position is not unlike the kind of tariff situations that are designed to protect any smaller industry in a smaller country.

You can very easily make the decision not to get in, and that may very well be the right decision for Canada. The fact is that Canada, through the creation of Telesat by the federal government several years ago, made the decision to be a pioneer in satellite communications, and has a good international record in achieving that. The world's first geo-stationary satellite was Canadian, and Canada's record in space has been very good.

The decision was clearly before the federal government and Telesat about a year and a half ago, when they had to make commitments as to whether they were going to opt for the next generation of satellite technology or fall back. And the decision was made that Canada was going to stay in the business. That decision having been made, the economies are such that without some protection, and you might as well use that word, you probably cannot compete with the size of the market that is available in Canada.

George Fierheller

Although I agree with a lot of things Mr. McMahon says, I do question that philosophy. I would even question the Canadian government's decision on that. It is all very well to talk about protecting Canadian technology, but it is a Hughes Aircraft-built satellite, launched from Cape Canaveral, on an American missile, and so on. I am not sure whose technology we are really trying to protect. If we are effectively making communications in Canada less competitive, then we could perhaps get them from other places. I also wonder whether that is to the benefit of many other industries and whether we could capitalize on it.

The problem with going into the satellite business in Canada is that if we are saying right now that we cannot compete with the United States because of the size of the market why did we go into it? We cannot market it anywhere, nobody else is going to buy it, and we have already said that the domestic market is too small to support it. Those are the kind of government-based decisions that I really do question. There is an incredible cost to the Canadian taxpayer, and yet it is hard to see where that technology is going for Canadians.

Andrew McMahon

There was one fundamental driving philosophy behind this, and I do not want to appear to be in the position of defending federal government decisions. A fundamental driving philosophy behind this is the question of service to the North in Canada, and there is no question that service is most effectively provided by satellite communication. In many cases, there is simply no alternative. That is something that weighs into the entire equation, in that it may be necessary to have almost as large an investment to provide such service and that the other things come incrementally. But I think that Canada, in some form or another, is committed to satellite communication as the only viable vehicle for effective communications to the North.

George Fierheller

Let me move on to the point I was going to make earlier, because if we are locked into that sort of thing at the present time, coming back to something that Gordon Thompson pointed out which I thought was very accurate, we are in danger, in this transborder area, of trying to freeze technology.

The talk I have heard seems to be to try to protect the fact that data are going to be largely stored in other countries, and therefore, we may loose control of it for whatever reasons. In the data processing industry, that may be flying in the face of a trend which is toward distributed processing, smaller computers, and so on. I think we have probably seen almost the end of this movement toward very large computers, at least for the time being. Their utilization will be for very specialized purposes and a lot of the work that is going to be done, and hence the records, will be stored on much smaller computers and on a much more localized basis. If you are concerned about the computer services industry, it is up to the computer services industry to recognize that trend and try to capitalize on it.

I am not so terribly concerned about the loss of jobs in Canada, because if the ability to move data processing cycles closer to the problem is in fact what is happening, then the requirements to have people locally to react to that by programming customized solutions, and so on, is going to be very great. The point that was made by Mr. Guedarian is that we are likely to be short of people to be able to implement the power that is being provided, not the other way around.

Chapter Three

Comments of Participants

Government is seeking places to control, regulate, and tax.

Transborder data flow is not a single issue, but rather a collection of interrelated issues.

The transborder data flow issues should be kept separate and dealt with individually.

It is essential that there be an over-view policy for the industry so that individual policies or legislation not appear piecemeal or contradictory.

A government focal point, such as the U.S. Office of Technology Assessment, should be considered.

Further legislation is not seen to be necessary at this time, especially if applied to an ill-defined problem.

It is important that impediments or barriers to placing more computers in Canada be removed.

Positive strategies, perhaps even subsidies, are required to further develop the computer and service industries in Canada.

The information processing industry needs special attention because of future potential and its ability to support other industries.

A shift to U.S. service bureaux is absolutely inevitable.

The best thing the government could do for employment is to train people in the trade or craft of programming, not the profession of programming.

Some people see domestic computer communications as another attempt to unify Canada, in the great tradition of the CBC, Air Canada, and so on.

If we, as users or suppliers of packet-switched services, do not know where the data are in the network, then that makes the data protection legislation in some countries a farce.

It would be cheaper to relocate our computers in the United States and provide our services to Canadians from there.

Is Canada *really* interested in having computers located in Canada?

Should we subsidize the import of computers into Canada?

We will do business where we can do it best.

Why build up a Canadian multinational only to have it do most of its work outside, where the market is?

Most of the problems associated with transborder data flows will become more apparent as information becomes a "private good."

While a possible loss of jobs in the short term is important, lost opportunity in the future is believed to be even more important.

Forecasts indicate continued loss of computer installations in Canada, even though technology permits centralized networks to be placed anywhere in North America.

Current policies discourage corporate data processing centres to locate here, and the service bureau industry could be the next example to relocate in the United States.

A Canadian presence in the information processing sector will ultimately be a political decision.

The information industry must become a national priority for it to continue to prosper.

With the proposed revision to the *Bank Act,* the crunch is here.

We need a clear-cut vision of where we are going in the communications field.

Why worry about independence in communications when industrial independence does not exist?

How could you tariff transborder data flows?

The real world will not wait for all the figures.

If another big contract came along, the attitude would be to say the hell with it because of problems in dealing with Canadian government regulations and boards.

A computing or corporate phenomenon?

There must be some focal point in government that has the power to recommend.

Government has become an agent concerned with its own survival, and is seeing an opportunity to become a principal actor in this transnational data flow area.

The major fear is not that corporations or enterprises will injure the little guy, but that government will sock it to everybody.

Is there really something happening which is of such magnitude as to suspend free trade and build indigenous capability?

Chapter Four

Workshop Reports and Commentary

George Fierheller, Systems Dimensions Ltd.

We had a very lively discussion, and we really made an effort to try to cover the five topics that were suggested, the first of which was the potential of growing dependence rather than interdependence. There was certainly a concern that government regulation was going to possibly lead to many more problems than, in fact, it was going to give solutions to. If that sounds like a bit of a recap of some of the things we were talking about this morning, that is probably right. We were not quite sure what the meaning of "growing dependence rather than interdependence" meant; but it lead to our asking the question of who called this meeting? Somebody turned and said, "Well, you know, it was not Frank Paine and the Honeywell people nor the manufacturers who wanted it, and it was not the services industry, and it certainly was not the common carrier, and so on," and we, in fact, came to the conclusion that the only people in Canada who were really pushing for any particular action in this field, at this point in time, happen to be the government. When we tried to come around to find out why the government should be so interested in coming up with regulations in this area, I am afraid we got a little on the cynical side. We came to the conclusion that (1) what you do not control, you cannot tax; and (2) if you cannot regulate it, then there is no need for a bureaucracy.

We then moved on to taking a look at item number two, which was the loss of employment opportunities. The point was made that, in fact, because there is not a computer manufacturing industry in Canada per se, loss of employment is not a major problem. It was also pointed out that computer manufacturing is becoming less and less labour intensive. There was a concern that perhaps loss of employment might happen for reasons that were not entirely related to the computer industry but because of a certain government attitude toward entrepreneurship in the country. There is a real concern that the taxation policy, at the present time, certainly does not encourage people to go out and start new enterprises in the country, and quite a variety of examples were given of that. There was a concern, as well, that regulation, as a growing Canadian industry in itself, was also leading to a strangling of a lot of new enterprises, and there were a few examples in that area. There was a further concern that regulation per se, particularly in the field of transborder data flows, might, in fact, discourage multinational corporations from operating in the country—the impact on employment could be far more than any potential loss of employment within the computer industry.

The point was also made that one of the real problems that we have in Canada right now is that there are not enough people capable of developing new applications in the computer field. The danger is certainly not unemployment in this industry, but simply a lack of enough qualified people coming out of our CEGEPs, community colleges, universities, whatever, to not only develop but market things that we already have. In general, the feeling of the group was that the loss of employment due to transborder data operations was not really the problem. The problem went much deeper than that.

The third area we talked about was the balance-of-payments problem. At that point, a comment was made that we should not put down the effect of multinational corporations operating in Canada, and that in fact a lot of them had been rather good at creating jobs in Canada, given the circumstances. Examples of Digital Equipment Corporation, IBM, and others were brought up. There were some comments, perhaps, about the wisdom of government in providing these kinds of organizations, which were very profitable and self-sufficient, with money to develop in Canada. That is to say, some of the loans made to some of the major companies a few years ago to develop in Canada may not really have been necessary. The observation was also made that the biggest deficiency in that sort of area was the lack of design capability in Canada, and design capability was the thing that discouraged multinationals from pulling out of the country. In other words, it was very easy to pull back manufacturing capability, but very difficult if there are major design projects which exist in the country, because you could not so easily move the people.

There was a comment made that the balance-of-payments problem certainly is a problem, and that the export of services could offset this. It was also suggested that Canada could produce good software products and could export these. Another comment was that Canada has developed quite a reputation in things like consulting engineering, and this in itself could provide a good sort of export market in communications and computer areas, and so on. But there is also the countervailing argument, which sounds a bit like the point made earlier, that unless the entrepreneurial environment turns out to be better in Canada than it is at the present time, the danger is that you will not simply export the services, you will also have the people leaving and the expertise with them.

The next area we took a look at was item four, the danger of loss of access to vital information. Someone commented in a slightly sarcastic way that he did not know there was any vital information in Canada anybody cared about. There is not an evident fear of losing our military secrets or something like that. The point was also made that this was not likely a vital problem, and there were not many examples people could come up with where, in fact, the loss of control of vital data had really been a problem. The conclusion was that the main reason the government wanted data available was simply to know where to tax operations, how to get after people who were violating the *Competition Act,* and so on. Other reasons that were not strictly economic could also provide an impetus.

The danger that decisions might end up being made by interest groups residing in another country was really viewed as being a sub-set of a much broader problem which went far beyond anything we have been talking about today. It really involves the whole concept that if Canada is largely a branch office economy you simply may not be able to stop this. No matter where you may access or how you may process data, if the head office of the company is in Holland, the United States, or wherever it happens to be, that is where the decisions are going to be made, and you have got to solve that problem, if you want to solve the other problems.

There was certainly a concern that if you tried to correct that simply by forcing multinational corporations to duplicate records in Canada or duplicate processing here, assuming that they are going to have to process eventually in their own head offices for consolidated reporting, and so on, all you are going to do is increase the costs in Canada of goods and services. This is going to have a continuing inflationary effect in the country and will simply decrease our productivity. The conclusion we came to is that it just does not make any sense to try to legislate against a good technological solution, because all you will do is get a poor economic solution.

The final comment, which I hardly need to add after you have heard all these other rather right-winged comments, was that the best government is the one where people are least aware of it.

Brendan McShane, consulting specialist

As far as item one was concerned, the potential of growing dependence rather than interdependence, we had the same problem as George Fierheller voiced—what was the meaning of that item? It was pointed out that it is mostly multinational flows that are responsible for this problem. We got into the mechanisms for controlling this, whether it should be voluntary enforcement, or even whether regulation was desirable. The group went into a small discussion at this point on the free flow of information as a concept, and whether it was viable in today's society. As you know, the free flow of information is a concept the United States has been responsible for since 1947, I believe. We questioned whether that concept is viable in today's economic world. Then we got into the question—does a nation have the right to restrict information? I think it was unanimous by all participants in the workshop that yes, it does.

We continued: if a nation does have the right to restrict information, how do you control it without oppressing it? We discussed the issue of cultural domination and economic links in cultural domination. Following this, we went beyond the pure cultural aspect of a domination to the economic dominations, if there be any. We did not resolve anything.

We became very analytical and tried to separate the main categories of information into a kind of taxonomy. We tried to categorize the information flows that were going back and forth, and discussed whether we should make it time-dependent on functional uses, or whether we should split it into major industries, and so forth. We did not really come to a conclusion there, but it was rather interesting. We went through the exercise to see if we could put some type of labels on the information flows as they were.

Then we had an *agent provocateur* from the Institute for Research on Public Policy ask if there was a relationship between the new technology and managerial styles. This provoked discussion on decentralization versus centralization, taxing policies and government style itself, cultural and political management styles, and the basis of information.

We also went off on a side discussion, which I found quite intriguing, about the *Bank Act* revision and the prohibitions extended to foreign data processing of customer records, and so on. The observation was made that previously it was not in report or legislation form, but that now Canadians were going to be faced with it directly—legislation on the prohibition of data processing in foreign data banks. It brought up the question that Canadians were immediately faced with a problem as far as that is concerned. I think we did sum up by saying that the United States and Canada do need each other, if we are talking about a free market economy in information. A lot of provisos as far as what a free market economy is, who can do what, and so on, were offered, but there was a natural link between the two economies.

As far as item two is concerned, the loss of employment opportunities, there was the observation that students are highly sensitive to job opportunities nowadays and are able to make the transitions, whereas maybe ten, fifteen, twenty years ago, they were not able to in the particular educational environments that existed then. But there was a consensus that there will be an absolute loss. How great the loss would be was not really delved into. We got into a discussion of how to make the tigers grow. Rather than looking at the negatives, we looked at how to turn this around to the positives, and how to make sure that there are job opportunities as opposed to job losses. One particular point during the discussion at this time was innovation as a key to Canada's future in this information world. Most of the participants kept coming back to the question of innovation and entrepreneurial management and the need for some new infusion, new capital in this area.

We also discussed differences between the industrial and information technology, and the uses between the two, which led back to innovation. When we talked about employment opportunities and loss of employment opportunities, we also got into a discussion of the levels of education of people, the terminal economy as opposed to the mainframe economy. We discussed managerial entrepreneurship with marketing strategies, and how to be innovative in this area, as far as the information flow was concerned. Gordon Thompson and I got into a discussion on communications and their role in the information economies, in the information industry itself, and we actually agreed to disagree on that point.

As to the third point, the addition to the balance-of-payments problem, Canada is consistent. But the nice thing about this was that there was a consensus that the time is ripe to make some innovative changes. This could be all sorts of possible programs, like the subsidization of mainframes to bring them into the country so as to sell services and information at a lower rate. This, again, is the question of innovation as far as software in marketing and managerial expertise for the information segment of the economy. The threat of government intervention in the market system was questioned. Government intervention was generally not wanted in this area, at this particular time.

We did not get through all the issues. We got to issue four, the danger of loss of legitimate access to vital information, and the observation was made that it is the perception that makes it real. But then the problem was that we do not know what is vital and what is not. Again, it is in the eyes of the beholder. One set of rules would apply, as one gentleman said, depending on whether it is my bank account or the oil companies'. If it is the oil companies', then we really want to look at their data, but if it is my bank account, no way! Again, a question of definition appeared—what is vital information and what is not vital information?

We did not get to five, which is probably the most provocative of the items, and I do not know what the participants would have said on that one. I dare not venture into that area.

Peter Robinson, Department of Communications, Canada

We were perhaps not as well behaved as the other two working groups in that we did not cover the five points of Mr. Faulkner. We had a wide ranging, free-for-all, no-holds-barred sort of discussion. In fact, at the beginning I was torn in three directions: (1) trying to be chairman; (2) trying to take notes; and (3) trying to defend myself. Somebody else volunteered to take the notes; what I am reflecting here is a brief summary that Daniel Cooper helped with and that he and I discussed afterwards.

First, what is so special about this information revolution, why are we so worried about it? We feel that the answer may be too complex to answer completely, but we can summarize fairly briefly. Information is in itself a major growth area, and it does provide an infrastructure for future growth and development in virtually all other areas of industrial activity. Therefore, there is a need to be concerned about it.

Transborder data flow is a compendium of interrelated issues, very few of which can merely be solved by legislation; what is needed, if anything is needed from government, is a tailor-made approach to dealing with the different issues involved. Most of my working group was very much concerned about the government getting its fingers on almost anything.

We did reach a conclusion, albeit with a bit of a dilemma: the government of Canada, and I suppose this would apply equally to the United States, does require an information infrastructure strategy. I have used information infrastructure strategy rather than an industrial strategy, because I believe that if you call it an industrial strategy, you get caught up with the traditional definitions of industry and this is not at all traditional. A rather long-term information infrastructure strategy is necessary for the Canadian government. Such a strategy will emphasize the positive in removing impediments, and so on, through looking at opportunities and de-emphasizing the problems. By putting emphasis on the positive side, most of the problems are going to disappear.

The second conclusion, which follows from the first, was that there appears to be a need for a competent over-view of this area, not so much from the viewpoint of developing all sorts of legislation and government intervention but to avoid the "ad hockery" in legislation that is now taking place (and these are not my words, but the words of the workshop), in the *Bank Act,* in the *Competition Act,* which touches on these issues, but appears to have focus within the government.

John M. Eger, attorney-at-law

We decided Canada should be a data haven, turning the nation into one large data base of operations, letting everyone migrate to jobs on farms and factories in the United States and elsewhere. Training the children to become programmers and analysts at about age seven would have a couple of results: Canada would have one very strong, viable industry, but because everyone had migrated, there would be no noise or air pollution, or environmental problems, and it would become the world's biggest tourist attraction because there would be no people. That is one scenario that really was not discussed at all, but it struck me very candidly when I first read Bill Cundiff's working paper, and I began to think about the data haven possibility as a national strategy.

We looked at the five issues or problems which Mr. Faulkner suggested accompany the phenomena of transborder data flow, and the sense was that he was portraying the negative. This was not the whole picture, and we accordingly discounted, at least *ab initio,* this set of problems that arise from the flow of data across national borders. In fairness, there was a minority view that it is a problem, that all of these issues raised are very serious ones, and that we are even willing, as a nation, to show our most nationalistic side, to accept a lesser standard of living, if after having been well thought out, it is decided that this is more important than letting technology and data flows wear away national borders.

Another view was that Mr. Faulkner, like all good politicians, was raising the problem, was grabbing for the jugular of public opinion, and was saying there are some problems that are coming, they are very real, they are not well defined, perhaps, but they do involve balance of payments, employment, inflation, and sovereignty or vulnerability, as a sub-set of sovereignty.

Having done that, the next thing we did was define the problems as narrowly as we could, within the constraints of time. What was the problem? Was it privacy? Not really; we can deal with privacy, if that is the problem. Perhaps there ought to be legislation; but legislation which narrowly protects the interest of one's individual right to control information about oneself. Was privacy a problem, then, in that sense? Perhaps if privacy were used as an economic weapon to deal with sovereignty, not privacy. In other words, a law passed for one purpose, misused or abused for another.

I do not think we defined the problem. We defined sets of issues, we defined clusters in which problems might arise, such as privacy, sovereignty, national security, extra-territoriality and jurisdiction, legal jurisdiction and economics, economic prowess. To the extent that we identified the problem, it was this—there is a problem, but we do not know how to define it. There was a genuine awareness that these statistics about the change in the economy, the information worker, the information-based economy, while not certain what the trends are, portray a very real event in our economic history within nation states and within the scheme of the international economy. Because of that and the fact that we are linked together by trade, among other reasons, there will be disruptions. There will be potential exacerbation of existing problems such as employment, balance of payments, and so on.

The next question we addressed was what to do about it. The answer there, as our ability to find the problem, was not very definitive. One suggestion was that there ought to be somebody in government, both in Canada and elsewhere, that we can look to for advice and co-ordination. We talked about Peter Robinson's office and what happened to it. No answer. We somewhat agreed that we really needed to ascertain with greater degree what the volume is. Had it really increased because of computers and communications, and if so, to what extent. What was the character of that change-over, five-year period? This, it was hoped, would provide some basis for further analysis. It may be important to determine through an in-depth analysis whether personal data flows are in jeopardy or whether there is a transfer of economic value that goes with the information, in which case you could then consider controls, if any.

The response to that was that governments will not wait. There already is something moving, there is an effort to develop legislation, to meet whatever this information revolution is presenting by way of challenges. The sense of the group and the sense of our hour-and-a-half was the fear that, yes, the clock was running away, somehow governments were running away proposing solutions to problems that had not yet been very well defined, either in the government sector or in the private sector.

Notwithstanding the desire to see governments slow down, to stay their hand until there was a better fix on what needed to be done, there was a desire to see this issue continually discussed in national and international forums, and for the dialogue to continue.

Appendix 1
Position Statements

Morris Crawford, U.S. State Department

One of the most consequential technological advances of modern times has been the development of the computer. Simultaneous advances in communications have given the computer a spatial dimension that greatly magnifies its impact on mankind and on international affairs. The result has been an explosive growth in the collection, manipulation, and use of information, and in recent years, a growing international appreciation of the value of information as a resource.

The phenomenal revolution of information technology has taken place largely unnoticed. The transformation into an "information society" has hardly attracted public attention. The economic efficiencies made possible by computer communications technology have been quietly absorbed, and the attractive new occupational opportunities have been happily welcomed. Only recently have governments and people begun to ponder the potential impact that the new technology may have on the lives of individuals.

We stand today on the threshold of exciting new applications of the computer communications technology, for instance, in electronic funds transfers and in electronic mail. We also can see on the horizon ahead even further new advances in computer and communications technology; advances in miniaturization and communication capacities that could lead to dramatic shifts in the structure of the world industry of computer communications from what it is today.

How can these new applications be brought into existence without undue economic disruptions or excessive dislocations in commonly accepted modes of life? In one form or another, this is a question that is being asked throughout the advanced western world today. Thus, the questions that are being asked by Canadians today are questions that people elsewhere are asking also, including Americans.

- What happens to jobs of postmen when mail begins to be transmitted electronically?
- Will bank tellers and book-keepers become obsolete and be displaced by automatic processing of bank monies?
- When technological information becomes "lost" in the electronic storage files of a monstrous and remote data bank, how can proprietary rights be exercised?
- What assurances can be given that improper usage will not be made of personal or proprietary data in a data bank?
- Does a clever computer software artist have a right to sell the results of a systematic data compilation made up from data innocently contributed for other purposes?

- Should the right to offer networking data services be open to all comers? Or should entry be controlled to serve traditionally defined public interests? Will traditional definitions of public interest remain adequate in tomorrow's "information" world?
- In a situation where the lines of distinction between computers and communications are all but obliterated, how can regulations that are designed to apply to either of the industries alone continue to be fairly enforced?

Some questions that are being raised today introduce new and strange concepts. "Technological sovereignty" and "information sovereignty" are baffling terms that are difficult to comprehend with any clear meaning. In Canada, the question is asked as to whether sovereign control is jeopardized when technical data on Canadian industry and industrial processes are stored in computer bases in the United States. In the United States, the question is asked whether the ease with which technological data can be exported abroad is enabling other nations to undermine the U.S. technological lead in certain industries. In both Canada and the United States, protectionist voices are heard arguing for the imposition of controls on the export of data.

All of the questions that I have referred to here have one thing in common. They all infer a value to data; they all imply that information is a resource that has value. If this is true, if "information is power" and has capacity to increase marketable production, should it not be treated as though it has worth? Should not information be marketed like any other factor of production?

These are not wholly new questions; it is the magnitude and overwhelming prevalence of information in today's world that is a new phenomenon. The world has long recognized the need for rules concerning the marketing of certain knowledge and information, even though it has not established universally accepted rules. Copyright and patent laws attest to this, and in a different sense the laws of libel also. Yet in an information age when some 40 per cent of U.S. gross national product arises in the information sector of the nation's economy, and an increasingly significant proportion is electronically transferred, questions of market value for information may not remain a matter for incidental concern. They may turn into issues of vital concern and become the heart of the matter.

Furthermore, given the ease of transborder data flows, the issue cannot be neglected internationally. Canada, as well as other countries, has vital information and transborder data interests. It is essential that international accommodations be sought that will provide reasonable satisfaction for national information interests. Such accommodations must not inhibit the application and development of computer communications technology. Computer communications technology should be viewed as today's most dynamic and effective factor of production, and be fully recognized for its contributions to improvements in the welfare and well-being of all nations.

While general international arrangements should be pressed, it is particularly essential that Canada and the United States establish acceptable means of assuring one another that information flow problems arising in the computer communications industries can be resolved to the mutual satisfaction of both countries.

John M. Eger, attorney-at-law

Within the next few years, national and international decisions and agreements will be made and legislation will be enacted by developed and developing countries that together will present a major threat to the world economy and to all nations increasingly dependent upon the free flow of information across national borders. If enacted or enforced primarily out of fear of abuse or by narrow self-interest, these regulations, laws, taxes, and tariffs dealing with privacy, security, censorship, sovereignty, or inherent property rights in data or information can severely restrict, if not block, the free flow of information throughout the world.

The need for international agreement on communications equipment and standards, communications tariffs, facilities planning, security, privacy, and confidentiality of information is acute. Yet there seems little likelihood that such agreement will be reached in the near term through existing forums or by present planning mechanisms. Moreover, the concerns, particularly those of the developing world, over the related issues of trade, technology transfer, foreign aid and assistance in computer communications and information technologies are likewise absent or barely visible from the policy-planning agenda of the world. Thus, as I stated in Brussels earlier this year:

> We are at a crucial juncture in world history; one where we can break the mold of our past by recognizing the serious limitations of conventional nation-state negotiations, and construct a new agenda to preserve and strengthen our democracies; or we can continue to plod from issue to issue, passing out laws, enforcing regulation, occasionally dealing decisively with the issues of the day, yet never grasping the essence of our actions in the larger theater of history. Counter to our efforts to approach this problem as any other—constructively, openly, aggressively—is perhaps a natural and understandable skepticism towards regulatory or legislative solutions of any kind.
>
> Yet, a fact of twentieth century life is that regulation can be good or bad, necessary or unnecessary, helpful or meddlesome. This we know of our personal experiences as citizens of every nation state. We, of course, support, even advocate, good regulation. Yet, on the international scale, we are slow to accept, urge, or even suggest regulation of any kind. Part of this is instinctive, part of it is a healthy distrust which sadly is not misplaced, but more, a great deal of our unwillingness arises from our failure to appreciate the size or shape of the world in which we live.

George Fierheller, Systems Dimensions Ltd.

In the computer field, a common problem is to start designing a system before the problem is defined. We are in danger of making the same mistake in transborder data flows. Pre-emptive legislation before the extent of the problem is really known could be detrimental to the development of better international understanding, the improvement of productivity, and may not result in any benefit to the computer industry within a country.

There are a number of issues which should be kept quite separate:
1. Protection of individual privacy. This is a legitimate responsibility of government, but involves only some kinds of data.
2. Protection of the local computer industry. It should be recognized that different countries develop different specialities, and a free-trade posture may benefit the industry and the countries involved.
3. National security. Again, this is a specialized area which can be treated by rifle shot rather than shotgun legislation.
4. Balance of payments. The main problem arises not from competition in the computer industry, but rather in the flow of work-load from branches in one country to head offices in another country. Again, this is an economic rather than a technological question and can be addressed by other means, that is, moral suasion on multinational corporations to be better corporate citizens.

The number of actual examples of abuses resulting from data being stored in another country is very small. The real impetus to most proposals for regulation are overtly commercial. In a country like Canada, which is very dependent on imported technology, prohibitions for narrow economic reasons could prove very counter-productive.

A PROPOSED APPROACH

1. Concentrate on the correction of abuses rather than a universal prohibition of data flows. An independent data ombudsman organization could look after any problems of individual rights within the country, and interface with similar organizations in other countries.
2. Concentrate on arranging international treaties for the extradition of data which may be stored in another country.
3. Allow data to be freely stored in countries where such mutual data extradition treaties exist.
4. Where no such treaties exist, the data ombudsman would require licences for the storage of data in such countries. Furthermore, there could be a requirement that such information be kept in duplicate within the source country's own borders.
5. If there are classes of information vital to national security, such information could be clearly designated in advance, and the government could specify that that particular information may not be held outside a country's borders.

In general, the default options should be the free flow of information, with only very specific prohibitions, and then only after there has been enough information gathered to indicate that such prohibitions are necessary. That information can be collected through the proposed data ombudsman operation.

J.C. Grant, Royal Bank of Canada

Over the past years, increasing numbers of organizations have developed effective communications networks that allow the transmission of data, both within their own country and across international borders.

The capability to transmit information has dramatically increased, and the associated time frames have diminished to the point where enormous quantities of data can be transmitted in a short time and at an economic cost. This has resulted in a change to the basic way organizations plan, design, and control their business and production operations.

In addressing the question of data flows, various categories of data can be seen to exist:
1. Data flows associated with meteorology, air transport control, and so on
2. Data flows associated with financial transactions carried out by financial institutions on behalf of their customers
3. Data flows associated with personal information on the health or credit worthiness of individuals
4. Data flows associated with original thinking, that is, results of research, software development programs, and so on
5. Data flows associated with planning, design, and control of enterprises, and so on

The impact upon Canada of certain of these categories of data being transmitted across its international boundaries can be significant, bearing in mind the large percentage of Canadian enterprises under foreign ownership and the high overhead cost of conducting business in Canada. Each category must be addressed separately, since the criteria or parameters for dealing with them are different. Transborder data flows concerned with meteorology information or those concerned with arranging international payments (the payment being a result of a previous decision) are quite different from transborder data flows concerned with the planning, design, and control of business enterprises. Planning, design, and control are becoming an increasingly larger component of the whole production process, particularly in the secondary industries, and as a result of technology, are rapidly becoming independent of the location where they are carried out.

Business enterprise, because of its competitive nature, tends to follow the path of least cost, especially when competing in the international market-place. In Canada, we have high overheads, largely resulting from government economic and social policies which tend to make us less competitive. Therefore, unless the environment for conducting business is improved, business enterprises in Canada face a dilemma which could result in more of the planning, design, and control functions moving out of high-cost locations and being relocated in more economic areas. Control of the actual production process, however, would continue to be exercised locally through the use of transborder data flows. An example of this in the financial industry relates to the treasurer's function for foreign subsidiaries operating in Canada. Information needed to carry out a large part of this function can be made available as easily in New York or Chicago as in Toronto or Montreal.

The implications of this are far reaching and may require legislative intervention to protect national and individual interests. A key problem area will be to define the limits of any such legislation so that desired results are achieved without further impacting business efficiency and the rights of individuals and organizations. The issue could possibly be resolved by compromise between business, various levels of domestic governments, and national governments, for example, by following precedents set in the tangible world where control is exercised by various means, including decisions made by businesses to be good national citizens, government persuasion, government tariffs, and other relatively straightforward mechanisms.

The different categories of data flows listed above are but a few of many categories. Others would address the jurisdictional and sovereignty issues, and so on; and while these issues are important, they are more easily resolved than the key issue of economics.

I hope solutions can be found outside of legislation, although the basic economic facts would suggest legislation may be the only answer.

Andrew McMahon, Bell Canada

The Computer Communications Group/TransCanada Telephone System (CCG/TCTS) recognizes the growing pressures for transnational data communications and the growing concerns about them. Canada has particular concerns vis-à-vis the United States because of its lower rates and high capacities. Notwithstanding, we favour an increased flow of transnational data communications consistent with sound national policies to maintain and promote Canadian data bases, to retain national communications paths within the country, and to protect the privacy and security of the data being transmitted.

1. Telecommunications can radically alter the way a society perceives itself and the world.
2. Modern technology is making it easier and cheaper to communicate internationally.
3. Growing concern about national security, privacy, employment, and technological colonization associated with transnational data flow.
4. Rate barriers to transnational data are an artifice to mask the lack of government policies in many countries.
5. Canadian policy of the common carriers—what it is, why it exists.
6. Canadian concerns—dumping of excess satellite capacity into Canada—routing through the United States would stunt indigenous Canadian industry—different laws in different nations affecting privacy and security—unequal rating concepts artificially restrict legitimate data flow.

7. Canada plays a leading role in international agencies, such as the Consultative Committee on International Telephone and Telegraph (CCITT), in developing world-wide standards.
8. Need for inter-networking, improving quality of service, through rates, end-to-end testing, agreements on network management.
9. The close co-operation with the United States has helped provide Canadians and Americans with excellent voice systems. We can do the same in the data field internationally, while recognizing each nation's legitimate desire to strengthen its domestic computer communications industries.
10. Properly addressed, transnational data flow is not a problem but an opportunity.

Brendan A. McShane, consulting specialist

The efficient and profitable management of any nation's international trade requires a continuing, timely, and relatively inexpensive flow of business data to and from all parts of the world. Both cost-efficient data transmission and data processing facilities are required to provide management with data in a form which can be used to make sound business decisions.

The importance of efficient transborder data flows to the conduct of modern-day business and international trade has to be kept in mind in evaluating the growing trend to emphasize the privacy aspects of transborder data flows. Balance must be struck to protect the privacy of personal information while allowing freedom of flow of non-personal information necessary to fulfil the legitimate and wide-ranging needs of society. It is hoped that any international agreement or convention, if adopted, will adequately assure such a balance.

The regulation of transborder data flows involves a number of separate, but interrelated, considerations and issues.

- The desire of nations to exercise national sovereignty in areas deemed important to their economic well-being or national security.
- The desire or requirement to preserve and protect the human rights and privileges of a nation's citizens.
- Pressures toward economic nationalism, undue favour to indigenous enterprises (whether state-owned or of the private sector), and the fostering or protection of domestic operations against international competition.
- The subject matter to be regulated must be clearly defined and thereby limited. "Personal data," for example, can be defined as information concerning only a *natural* person, or it can be defined more broadly so as to include any *legal* person. The broader definition could enable government agencies to "control" the flow of *commercial* (as distinct from personal) information, such as pay-roll processing and export/import documentation.
- The transmission of data and all kinds of information across national borders (airline and hotel reservations, bank deposits, telephone conversations, books and magazines, pay-roll records, documents relating to commercial offers,

bids, acceptances, contracts, and so on) will grow at an increasing rate. The practice of transmitting international trade data electronically for the efficient and low cost provision of trade information and documentation is only one example of such growth of new technology contributions. It could be a disservice to all nations and people to impede or inhibit the free flow of information needed for international commerce through data protection or privacy regulations that would go beyond the specific objectives that require protection or regulation.

- The establishment of controls over international transfer of data, if of an inhibiting nature, might require major reorganization of multinational data processing operations. The relationships of data processing services and data processing organizations and their customers, and the differences or responsibilities between such services and the users of such information should be carefully provided for.
- Licensing confers wide and often arbitrary powers on the regulatory agency to determine how extensively, in substance and administration, personal privacy legislation will be applied. There are other less restrictive and capricious alternatives to such legislation. Development of voluntary standards governing data storage and transmission techniques and methods is eminently feasible. When coupled with fair information practices by users through self-regulation, a mechanism for protection of individual rights against abuse comes into place. What requires protection from abuse is the privacy rights of natural persons, not the operating techniques of data transmission and information processing and their associated technologies.
- Some current and proposed legislation would regulate data security. The licensing agency would be given authority to issue regulations on data security. Such legislation would, in effect, regulate technological development and technical operating methodologies in order to prevent abuse. The appropriateness of such legislation and regulations in guaranteeing security measures is questionable because of the range of software and hardware applications, data variations, and physical environments in which systems operate.
- It is necessary that national laws in this area be selectively harmonized and made consistent. However, the variations in restriction, regulation, and nationalistic exclusivity surrounding the proposed legislation in foreign countries would create severe operational problems for those planning the usage and technology of information systems which rely on central and local data bases, electronic modes of printing, and/or telecommunications for the crossing of national boundaries. At a minimum, these proposed laws would make both data transmissions and data processing more costly to all and thus unnecessarily inefficient. In some instances, these proposals would effectively bar the utilization of electronic data processing systems without, however, preventing possible abuses to personal privacy by other (for example, manual) means in either national or transborder communications.

- Certain tariff and non-tariff measures applied, or proposed to be applied, by various countries to information or such organizations as Euronet are, or would be, unreasonable.
- Discrimination in the pricing and availability of telecommunications facilities and services by governmental monopolies in order to make transborder data processing abroad economically non-competitive, if not actually impossible.
- Import and export duties on data transmitted for processing abroad, as if the data itself constituted a dutiable product.
- Onerous and economically burdensome requirements in import and export licences mandated for the cross-border transmission of data, or prohibitive conditions, such as requirements for the local retention of copies of all data transmitted for processing abroad, and for the posting of security bonds or deposits to guarantee compliance abroad with domestic requirements.

It is thus apparent that many of the proposed rules and regulations being considered or already in effect in other countries go far beyond a proper and balanced concern for protection of rights of personal privacy.

The foregoing comments are premised largely on the needs of typical international commercial enterprises. In addition, the special, but very important, needs of businesses such as broadcasting, printed news, publishing, motion pictures, and recording must also be considered. These more specialized areas have their own particular relationship to issues of privacy, censorship, right of access, channel rights, taxation, and distribution. These areas, of course, also require a reasonable balance between protection of privacy and freedom of information flow.

Peter Robinson, Department of Communications, Canada

I should preface these notes by emphasizing that they do not represent an official position of the Canadian government nor of any of its departments or agencies.

The issue of personal privacy is important, and transborder data flows, even between Canada and the United States, could be influenced by legislative action in Europe and by international agreements that might arise from current work in the OECD and in the Council of Europe.

However, I would like to direct attention to what has been described as the "strategic" issues.

The Canadian government's Green Paper on Computer/Communications Policy expressed concern about:

> . . . the problems involved in exercising Canadian jurisdiction over companies operating in Canada which store and process business data outside the country . . . . the role of multinational corporations in the computer/communications field which in turn touches upon general economic policy.

The report of the Task Force on Privacy and Computers concluded that:

> The principal problem . . . is not one of the privacy of Canadian data subjects being invaded by data about them stored in the United States. It is rather that data processing and communications business may be lost to Canadians as a result of this foreign flow; that data in United States data banks might be peremptorily withheld abroad for a variety of reasons, including security regulations, court injunctions, etc.; that United States laws might change and leave Canadians less well protected; and that, as a sovereign state, Canada feels some national embarrassment and resentment over increasing quantities of often sensitive data about Canadians being stored in a foreign country.

In considering these and other concerns, a number of legal questions arise:
1. With regard to access to information, many countries have laws regarding disclosure; and legislation in one country is sometimes in conflict with legislation in another. In these cases, companies storing records abroad risk being in breach of one law or the other.
2. Many Canadian statutes, federal and provincial, contain provisions for the maintenance of books of account and other records in Canada. It is not clear whether computer print-outs received in Canada from foreign locations, where the records are stored and processed, are sufficient in all cases as a method of compliance with these statutory requirements.
3. A number of acts related to the issue of a licence or a permit allow the responsible minister to impose constraints which could impact on transborder data flows.
4. Some acts empower seizure of records and books of account to provide evidence in court proceedings. This raises questions as to what is really meant by ''books of account'' and what would be allowable as evidence.
5. Authentication of documents transmitted electronically also raises a number of legal questions.

Of particular concern are the possible economic impacts of transborder data flows. There is evidence of an increasing migration of information processing activities from Canada to the United States. Current estimates suggest that Canada will import about $350 million worth of information processing services this year—a doubling over the past three years. The estimates further suggest that this could increase to some $1.5 billion by 1985.

If it materializes, this could have an important impact on Canada's balance of payments and on Canadian job opportunities in a high technology area. Today it is estimated that the number of jobs created abroad, rather than in Canada, to meet Canadian needs for information storage and processing amounts to about seventy-five hundred; this could rise to twenty-three thousand by 1985.

A further factor contributing to concern about the jobs exported through use of foreign computing services is that it is not uncommon for many users of the services—managers, accountants, planners, and management support personnel—to be consolidated at head offices along with the major computing activity. The out-flow of employment could therefore be much greater than the number of information processing workers directly involved.

In our present approach to deal with these questions and issues, we will need to take into account the following requirements:
1. Data protection and other legal measures must not restrict unnecessarily the efficiency, versatility, or innovative capabilities of the private or public sectors.
2. Both sectors must be permitted to adapt their functional and organizational structures to the on-going automation of information processing and information transfer activities.
3. Any action taken must be reconcilable with social, legal, and economic realities, and changes must satisfy constitutional and other legal requirements, be politically acceptable, and should not harm individuals or the institutions of society.

Unfortunately these requirements are not always compatible. It will therefore be a matter of assessing the advantages and disadvantages of various possible approaches, and selecting that which appears to lead to the maximum net gain.

I have concentrated here on the problems associated with transborder data flows, but I should not end without acknowledging that there are also a number of benefits. However, it is the problems that we must get out on the table for discussion; we must weigh the potential dangers and disadvantages against the benefits; and we must attempt to resolve the problems without negative impact on the advantages.

Appendix 2
List of Participants

Donald M. Atkinson
Director
Long Range Planning
Bell Canada
Chaudière Terrasses
5th Floor
25 Eddy Street
Hull, Quebec
J8X 4B5

Dr. Ellen Baar
Assistant Professor
Division of Social Sciences
York University
4700 Keele Street
Downsview, Ontario
M3J 1P3

Gaston Beauséjour
Sous-ministre adjoint
Ministère des Communications
Edifice G, 3e étage de la tour
675, boul. Saint-Cyrille
Québec, Québec
G1R 4Y7

Robert J. Bolton
Manager, Marketing & Development
Geodigit
500, 404-6th Avenue S.W.
Calgary, Alberta
T2P 0R9

Jay Bryan
Reporter
Business & Finance Section
The Montreal Gazette
Montreal, Quebec
H3C 3R7

W.H. Calder
Vice-President
FRI Information Service Ltd.
Suite 600
1801 McGill College Avenue
Montreal, Quebec
H3A 2N4

---

* Panelist

R.A. Callahan
Manager — Carrier Relations
Téléglobe Canada
680 Sherbrooke Street West
Montreal, Quebec
H3A 2S4

Robert H. Conn
Arthur Andersen & Co.
1666 K Street, N.W.
Washington, DC 20006

Daniel Cooper
McCarthy & McCarthy
P.O. Box 48
Toronto-Dominion Centre
Toronto, Ontario
M5K 1E6

Dr. A.J. Cordell
Science Adviser
Science Council of Canada
150 Kent Street, 7th Floor
Ottawa, Ontario
K1P 5P4

Eric Cowan
Privy Council Office
Government of Canada
Ottawa, Ontario
K1A 0A3

* Morris Crawford
Acting Director
Office of Bilateral and Multilateral Science
    and Technology Programs
U.S. Department of State
Room 4327
Washington, DC 23007

* W.E. Cundiff
Senior Research Associate
Futures Studies Program
Institute for Research on Public Policy
3535 Queen Mary Road, Suite 514
Montreal, Quebec
H3V 1H8

Pat Dowling
TransCanada Telephone System
160 Elgin Street - 9th Floor
Ottawa, Ontario
K2P 2C4

* John M. Eger
Attorney-at-Law
1742 N Street, N.W.
Washington, DC 20036

* George Fierheller
President
Systems Dimensions Ltd.
770 Brookfield Road
Ottawa, Ontario
K1V 6J5

Oswald H. Ganley
Research Associate
J.F. Kennedy School of Government
Program Information Resources Policy
Harvard University
200 Aiken Avenue
Cambridge, MA 02138

Thomas F. Goldman
Vice-President
TRW Credit Data
505 City Parkway West
Orange, CA 92668

Ken Gordon
Information Systems Manager
Digital Equipment of Canada Ltd.
P.O. Box 11500
Kanata, Ontario
K2H 8K8

Calvin C. Gotlieb
Professor
Department of Computer Science
University of Toronto
Toronto, Ontario
M5S 1A7

* J.C. Grant
Assistant General Manager
Systems Development
Royal Bank
1 Place Ville Marie
Montreal, Quebec
H3C 3A9

Robert Greer
Manager
Information Systems Department
Duplate Canada Ltd.
50 St. Clair Avenue West
Toronto, Ontario
M4V 1M9

———

* Panelist

George Guedarian
CBS
385 Madison Avenue
New York, NY 10017

Geoffrey D. Hampson
General Manager
Information Systems Division
Systems Approach Ltd.
350 Sparks Street
Suite 605
Ottawa, Ontario
K1R 7S8

Steven A. Hilchen
Advisor, Telecommunications Policies
Data Services
Control Data Corporation
500 West Putnam Avenue
Greenwich, CT 06830

Dr. David Hoffman
Director
Futures Studies Program
Institute for Research on Public Policy
3535 Queen Mary Road, Suite 514
Montreal, Quebec
H3V 1H8

Alexandra E. Karlow
Government Issues Analyst
American Express Company
1700 K Street N.W.
Washington, DC 20006

J.E. Kavanah
Manager, Int'l D.P.
Computing & Telecommunications Services
Union Carbide Corporation
Old Saw Mill River Road, Route 100C
Tarrytown, NY 10591

Barry D. Klett
Market Planning
Computel Systems Ltd.
1200 St. Laurent Blvd.
Ottawa, Ontario
K1K 3Y4

Gary Kreps
Research Assistant
Futures Studies Program
Institute for Research on Public Policy
3535 Queen Mary Road, Suite 514
Montreal, Quebec
H3V 1H8

Participants / **87**

Jean Labelle
Directeur
Services en logiciel
L'Industrielle-Services Techniques Inc.
2, complexe Desjardins
Montréal, Québec
H5B 1B3

Gordon Lloyd
Canadian Manufacturers' Association
One Yonge Street
Toronto, Ontario
M5E 1J9

W.H. Loewen
President
Comcheq Services Limited
499 Portage Avenue
Winnipeg, Manitoba
R3B 2E3

Jacques Lyrette
Directeur
Gestion des programmes de recherche
Politique et planification de la recherche
Ministère des Communications
Edifice Journal Nord
300, rue Slater
Ottawa, Ontario
K1A 0C8

Paul Marier
Reporter
Computing Canada
63 Fourth Avenue
Verdun, Quebec
H4G 2X9

Ronald J. McAdam
Policy Director
Canadian Telecommunications
　Carriers Association
1 Nicholas Street
Suite 700
Ottawa, Ontario
K1N 7B7

David G. McIntosh
Manager
Product Planning & Development
Information Services
Canadian General Electric
1420 Dupont Street
Toronto, Ontario
M6H 2B2

* A.M. McMahon
Vice-President
Computer Communications
Bell Canada
160 Elgin Street, F11
Ottawa, Ontario
K1G 3J4

* Brendan A. McShane
Consulting Specialist
Information Services
9303 Jesup Lane
Bethesda, MD 20014

Horace Miles
Supervisor
Programming & Technical Development
PPG Industries, Inc.
One Gateway Center
Pittsburgh, PA 15222

Maurice A. Morin
Président
Les Informaticiens associés de Montréal Inc.
3414, avenue du Parc, bureau 321
Montréal, Québec
H2X 2H5

J.M. Neelands
Manager
Computing and Telecommunications
Union Carbide Canada Limited
123 Eglinton Avenue East
Toronto, Ontario
M3P 1J3

Jack L. Osborn
Regulatory Compliance Manager
TRW Credit Data
505 City Parkway West
Orange, CA 92668

Bruce Outzen
General Tire & Rubber
1 General Street
Akron, OH 44329

Frank Paine
Corporate Consultant —
Telecommunications
Honeywell Information System
2025 Sheppard Avenue East
Willowdale, Ontario
M2J 1V6

---

* Panelist

Angeline Pantages
International Editor & Bureau Manager
Datamation
35 Mason Street
Greenwich, CT 06830

Dr. J.C. Paradi
President
Dataline Systems Ltd.
175 Bedford Road
Toronto, Ontario
M5R 2L2

Michael J. Quinn
The Intergroup Partnership
287 Macpherson Avenue
Toronto, Ontario
M4V 1A4

John M. Regan
National Sales Manager
Call/370 Management
Time-Sharing Services
Control Data Canada Ltd.
50 Hallcrown Place
Willowdale, Ontario
M2J 1P7

Mado Reid
Associate Editor
Futures Studies Program
Institute for Research on Public Policy
3535 Queen Mary Road, Suite 514
Montreal, Quebec
H3V 1H8

* Dr. Peter Robinson
Policy Adviser
Computer/Communications
Department of Communications
300 Slater Street
Ottawa, Ontario
K1A 0C8

Robert Russel
President
Orbafilm Limited
17 Côte Ste-Catherine Road
Montreal, Quebec
H2V 1Z7

Gerson Safran
Director
Consulting and Support Services
Management Horizons Data Systems
257 Adelaide Street South
London, Ontario
N5Z 3K7

Glenn Ste-Croix
Technical Services Specialist
Abbott Laboratories Ltd.
5400 Côte de Liesse Road
Montreal, Quebec
H3C 3K6

Ian P. Sharp
President
I.P. Sharp Associates, Limited
145 King Street West
Toronto, Ontario
M5H 1J8

James G. Smith
Senior Consultant to C.I.S.
Inco Limited
1 First Canadian Place
Toronto, Ontario
M5X 1C4

Paul Smith
SEI Corporation
Valley Ford Executive Mall
Building 7
680 East Swedesford Road
Wayne, PA 19037

Hollis Sobers
Senior Consultant
Allied Chemical Corporation
P.O. Box 1039 R
Morristown, NJ 07960

Norman Song
President
Boeing Computer Services Canada, Ltd.
134 Abbott Street
Vancouver, British Columbia
V6B 2K4

Claude Tessier
Chroniqueur
Recherche et Technologie
Le Soleil
Québec, Québec
G1K 7J6

---

* Panelist

Gordon B. Thompson
Manager
Communication Studies
Bell Northern Research
P.O. Box 3511
Station C
Ottawa, Ontario
K1Y 4H7

J.W. Valentine
Manager
Hardware Planning & Telecommunications
Datacrown Limited
650 McNicoll Avenue
Willowdale, Ontario
M2H 2E1

J.M. Vaughn
Director, Division Systems
Glass Information Systems
PPG Industries, Inc.
One Gateway Center
Pittsburgh, PA 15222

J.S. Wightman
IBM Canada
150 Laurier West
Ottawa, Ontario
K1N 8X1

Russell Wilkins
Research Associate
Futures Studies Program
Institute for Research on Public Policy
3535 Queen Mary Road, Suite 514
Montreal, Quebec
H3V 1H8

Zavis P. Zeman
Project Leader
Futures Studies Program
Institute for Research on Public Policy
3535 Queen Mary Road, Suite 514
Montreal, Quebec
H3V 1H8

Mr. Zucker
Director Telecom
CBS
51 West 52nd Street
New York, NY 10019

RAYMOND H. FOGLER LIBRARY
DATE DUE